GOD'S PROMISES

SALO

DEVOTIONAL FOR MEN

Weekly Devotional Table of Contents

This Devotional uses 31 of God's Promises from the Bible and is designed as a weekly format with each week having one focus Promise. There is also a prompter question or discussion point related to the Promise to help you get focused on how to apply the Promise to your daily life. The remainder of the week you will be prompted using the SALO (Stop, Ask, Listen, Obey) method with each day focusing on one aspect of SALO. You will also be able to journal your thoughts each day. The SALO method is discussed in depth in my book: **_Loving Conversations: How to Pray and Hear God's Voice._**

Even if you haven't read the book, this Devotional format is easy to follow and helps you to reflect on His word throughout your week and develop your relationship with Him.

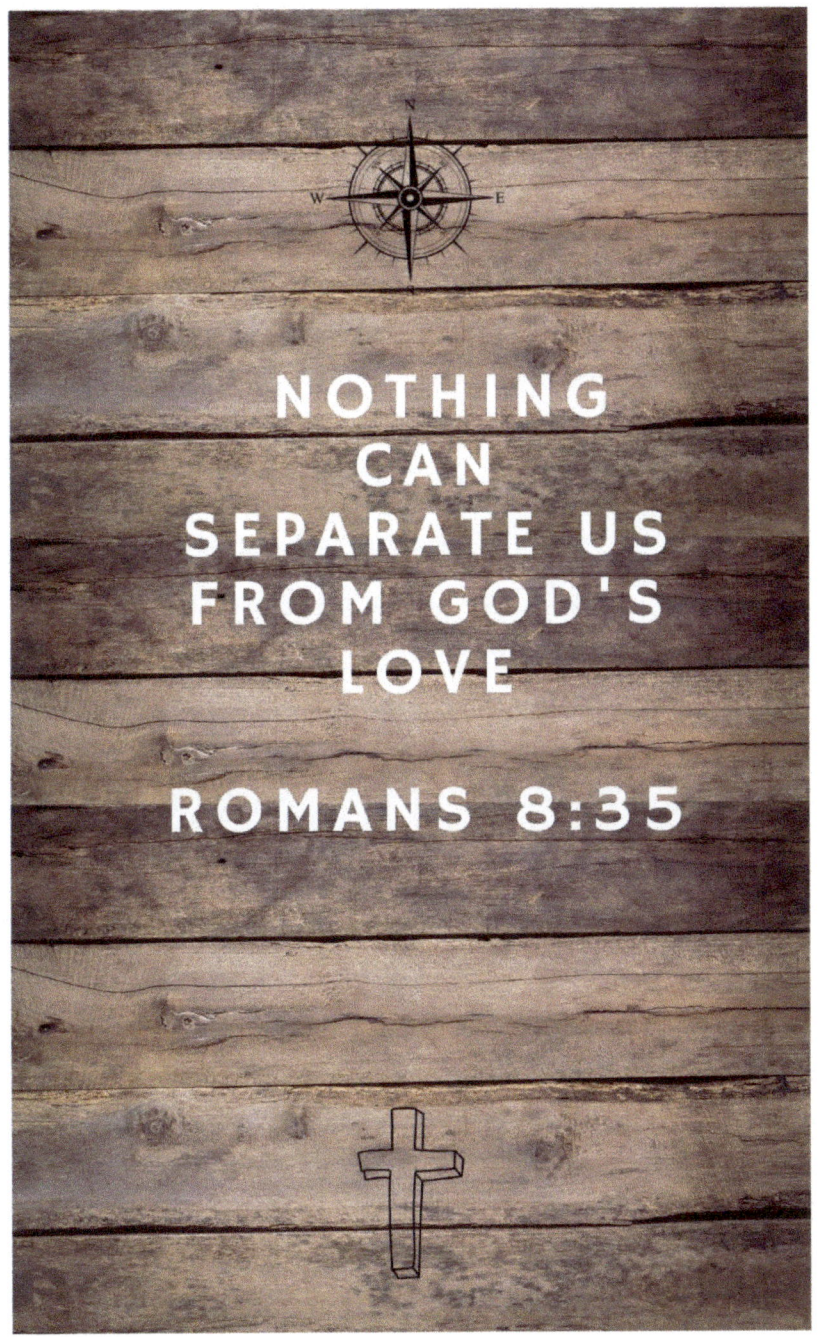

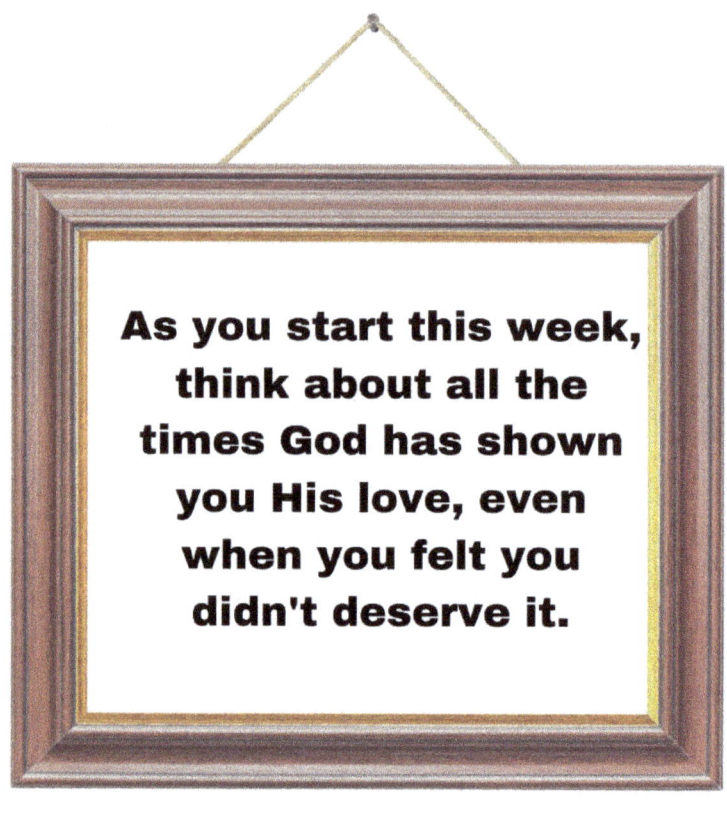

As you start this week, think about all the times God has shown you His love, even when you felt you didn't deserve it.

STOP...

JOURNAL TO THE LORD ABOUT WHAT THIS PROMISE MEANS TO YOU. WHY IS THIS PROMISE IMPORTANT?

ASK...

ASK THE LORD ABOUT HOW THIS PROMISE APPLIES TO YOUR LIFE RIGHT NOW. SPEAK FROM THE HEART ABOUT WHY YOU ARE ASKING.

OBEY...

HOW CAN I APPLY WHAT THE LORD HAS TOLD ME INTO MY LIFE CONSISTENTLY GOING FORWARD?

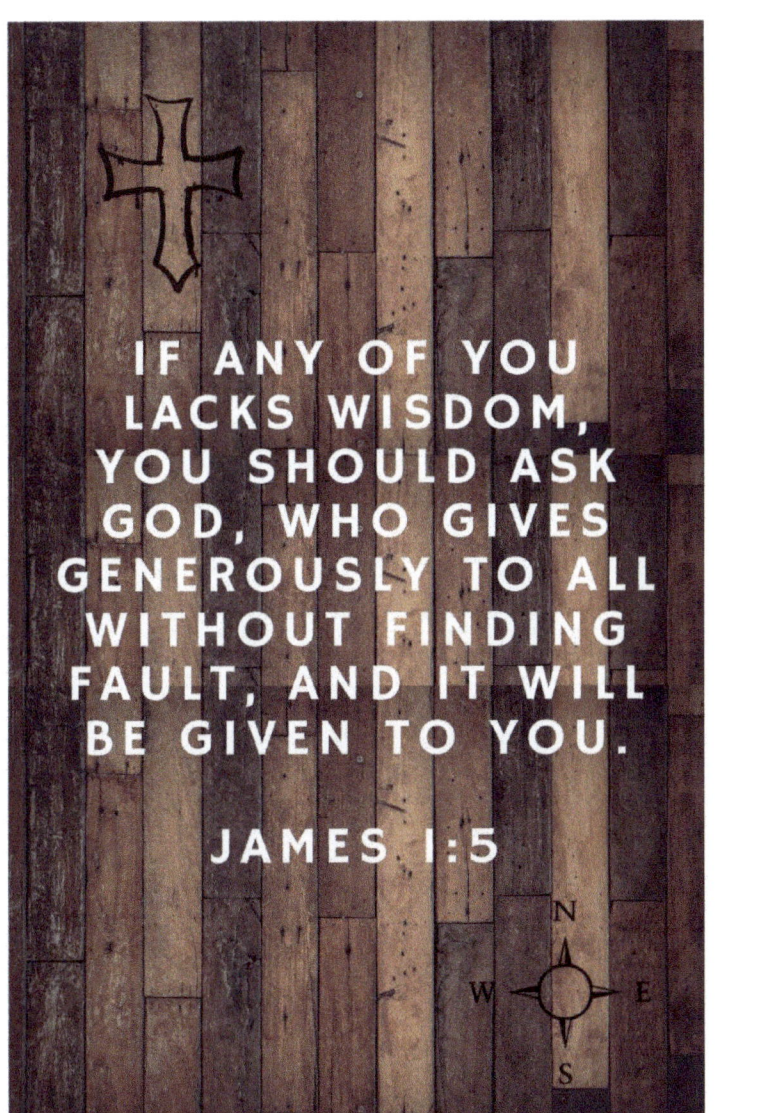

This week really focus on those times you know God gave you guidance and how can you live your life like that everyday with Him.

STOP...

JOURNAL TO THE LORD ABOUT WHAT THIS PROMISE MEANS TO YOU. WHY IS THIS PROMISE IMPORTANT?

ASK...

ASK THE LORD ABOUT HOW THIS PROMISE APPLIES TO YOUR LIFE RIGHT NOW. SPEAK FROM THE HEART ABOUT WHY YOU ARE ASKING.

OBEY...

HOW CAN I APPLY WHAT THE LORD HAS TOLD ME INTO MY LIFE CONSISTENTLY GOING FORWARD?

THEN YOU WILL
CALL ON ME AND
COME AND PRAY
TO ME, AND I WILL
LISTEN TO YOU.

JEREMIAH 29:12

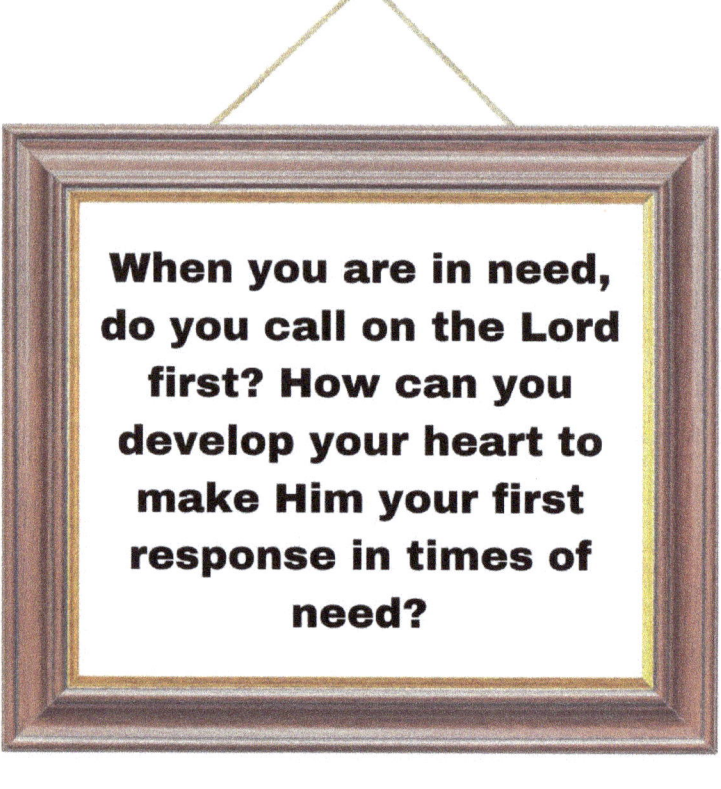

When you are in need, do you call on the Lord first? How can you develop your heart to make Him your first response in times of need?

STOP...

JOURNAL TO THE LORD ABOUT WHAT THIS PROMISE MEANS TO YOU. WHY IS THIS PROMISE IMPORTANT?

ASK...

ASK THE LORD ABOUT HOW THIS PROMISE APPLIES TO YOUR LIFE RIGHT NOW. SPEAK FROM THE HEART ABOUT WHY YOU ARE ASKING.

OBEY...

HOW CAN I APPLY WHAT THE LORD HAS TOLD ME INTO MY LIFE CONSISTENTLY GOING FORWARD?

"TRUST IN THE LORD
WITH ALL YOUR
HEART AND LEAN 'NOT
ON YOUR OWN
UNDERSTANDING; IN
ALL YOUR WAYS
SUBMIT TO HIM, AND
HE WILL MAKE YOUR
PATHS STRAIGHT."

PROV 3:5-6

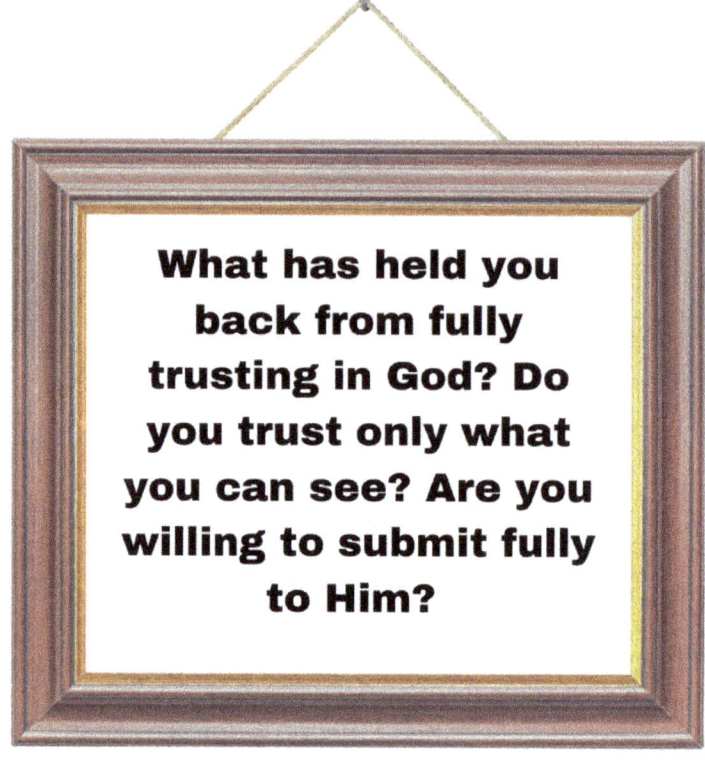

What has held you back from fully trusting in God? Do you trust only what you can see? Are you willing to submit fully to Him?

STOP...

JOURNAL TO THE LORD ABOUT WHAT THIS PROMISE MEANS TO YOU. WHY IS THIS PROMISE IMPORTANT?

ASK...

ASK THE LORD ABOUT HOW THIS PROMISE APPLIES TO YOUR LIFE RIGHT NOW. SPEAK FROM THE HEART ABOUT WHY YOU ARE ASKING.

OBEY...

HOW CAN I APPLY WHAT THE LORD HAS TOLD ME INTO MY LIFE CONSISTENTLY GOING FORWARD?

TAKE DELIGHT IN
THE LORD, AND HE
WILL GIVE YOU THE
DESIRES OF YOUR
HEART.

PS 37:4

STOP...

JOURNAL TO THE LORD ABOUT WHAT THIS PROMISE MEANS TO YOU. WHY IS THIS PROMISE IMPORTANT?

ASK...

ASK THE LORD ABOUT HOW THIS PROMISE APPLIES TO YOUR LIFE RIGHT NOW. SPEAK FROM THE HEART ABOUT WHY YOU ARE ASKING.

OBEY...

HOW CAN I APPLY WHAT THE LORD HAS TOLD ME INTO MY LIFE CONSISTENTLY GOING FORWARD?

AND GOD IS ABLE
TO BLESS YOU
ABUNDANTLY, SO
THAT IN ALL
THINGS AT ALL
TIMES, HAVING ALL
THAT YOU NEED,
YOU WILL ABOUND
IN EVERY GOOD
WORK.

2 COR 9:8

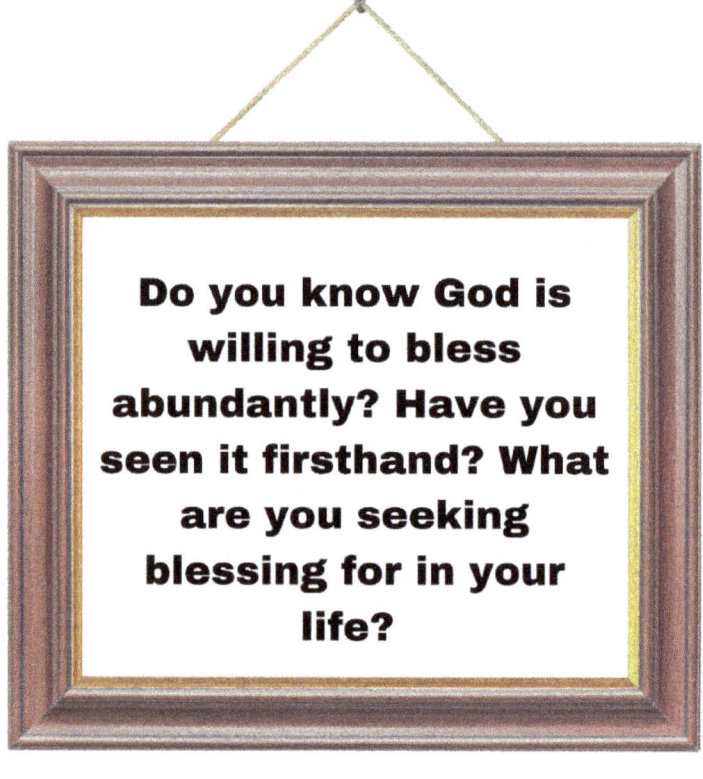

Do you know God is willing to bless abundantly? Have you seen it firsthand? What are you seeking blessing for in your life?

STOP...

JOURNAL TO THE LORD ABOUT WHAT THIS PROMISE MEANS TO YOU. WHY IS THIS PROMISE IMPORTANT?

ASK...

ASK THE LORD ABOUT HOW THIS PROMISE APPLIES TO YOUR LIFE RIGHT NOW. SPEAK FROM THE HEART ABOUT WHY YOU ARE ASKING.

OBEY...

HOW CAN I APPLY WHAT THE LORD HAS TOLD ME INTO MY LIFE CONSISTENTLY GOING FORWARD?

WHICH OF YOU, IF YOUR
SON ASKS FOR BREAD, WILL
GIVE HIM A STONE? OR IF
HE ASKS FOR A FISH, WILL
GIVE HIM A SNAKE? IF YOU,
THEN, THOUGH YOU ARE
EVIL, KNOW HOW TO GIVE
GOOD GIFTS TO YOUR
CHILDREN, HOW MUCH
MORE WILL YOUR FATHER
IN HEAVEN GIVE GOOD
GIFTS TO THOSE WHO ASK
HIM!

MT 7:9-11

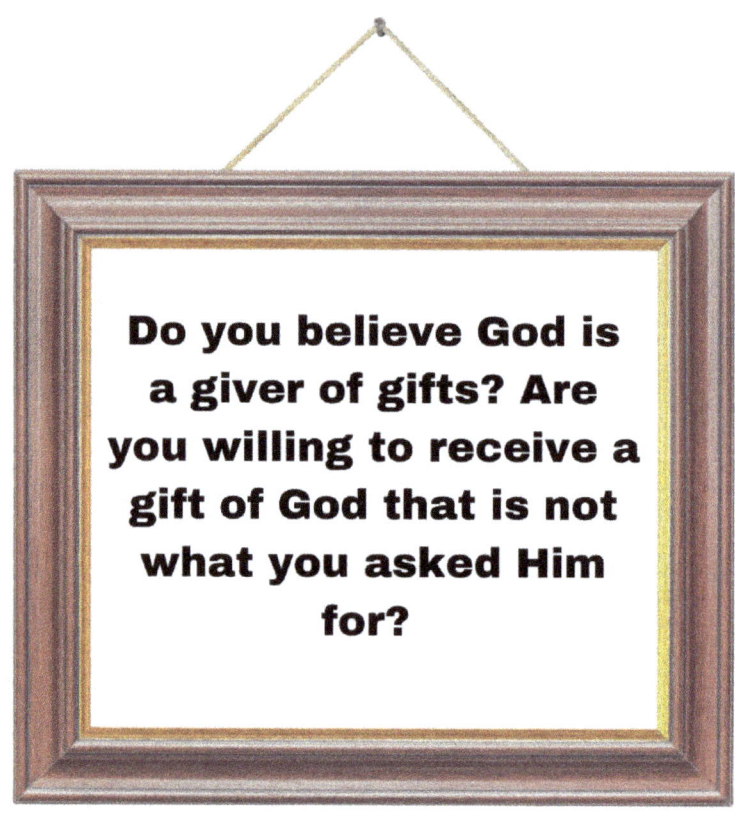

Do you believe God is a giver of gifts? Are you willing to receive a gift of God that is not what you asked Him for?

STOP...

JOURNAL TO THE LORD ABOUT WHAT THIS PROMISE MEANS TO YOU. WHY IS THIS PROMISE IMPORTANT?

ASK...

ASK THE LORD ABOUT HOW THIS PROMISE APPLIES TO YOUR LIFE RIGHT NOW. SPEAK FROM THE HEART ABOUT WHY YOU ARE ASKING.

OBEY...

HOW CAN I APPLY WHAT THE LORD HAS TOLD ME INTO MY LIFE CONSISTENTLY GOING FORWARD?

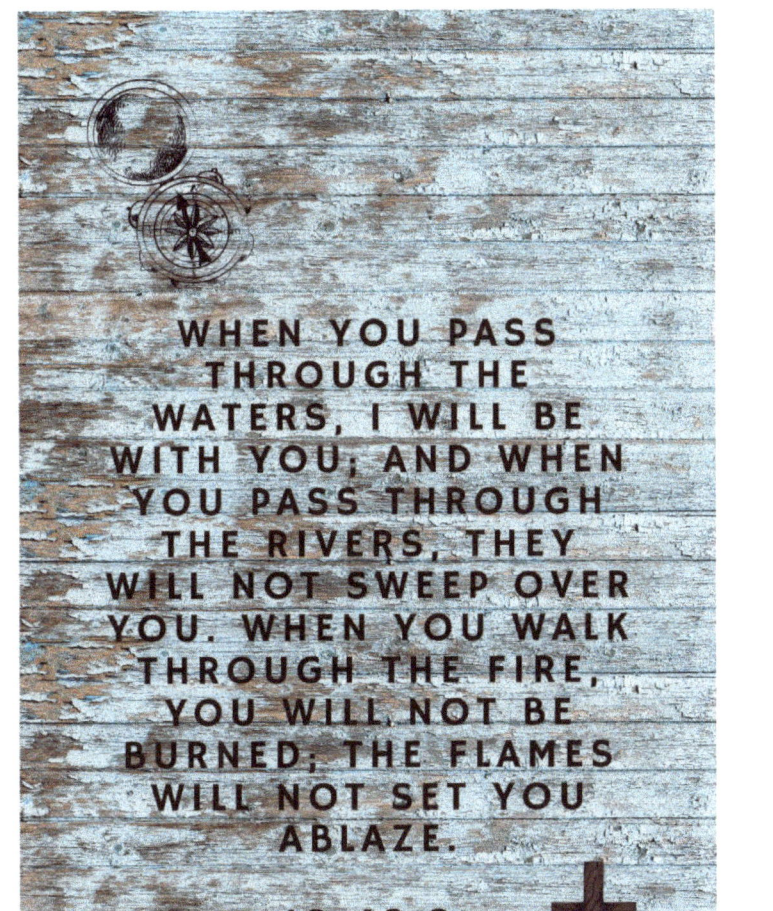

WHEN YOU PASS
THROUGH THE
WATERS, I WILL BE
WITH YOU; AND WHEN
YOU PASS THROUGH
THE RIVERS, THEY
WILL NOT SWEEP OVER
YOU. WHEN YOU WALK
THROUGH THE FIRE,
YOU WILL NOT BE
BURNED; THE FLAMES
WILL NOT SET YOU
ABLAZE.

IS 43:2

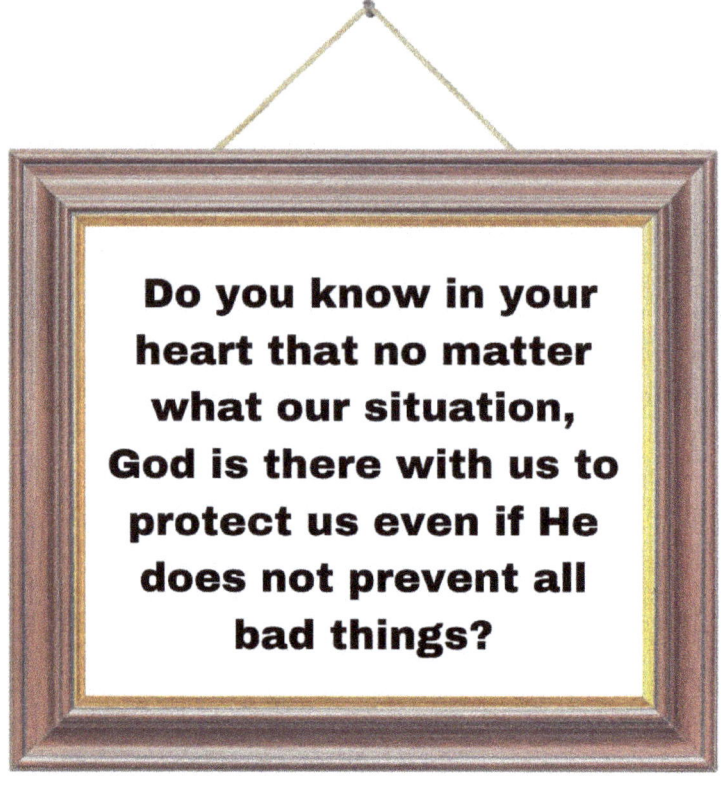

Do you know in your heart that no matter what our situation, God is there with us to protect us even if He does not prevent all bad things?

STOP...

JOURNAL TO THE LORD ABOUT WHAT THIS PROMISE MEANS TO YOU. WHY IS THIS PROMISE IMPORTANT?

ASK...

ASK THE LORD ABOUT HOW THIS PROMISE APPLIES TO YOUR LIFE RIGHT NOW. SPEAK FROM THE HEART ABOUT WHY YOU ARE ASKING.

OBEY...

HOW CAN I APPLY WHAT THE LORD HAS TOLD ME INTO MY LIFE CONSISTENTLY GOING FORWARD?

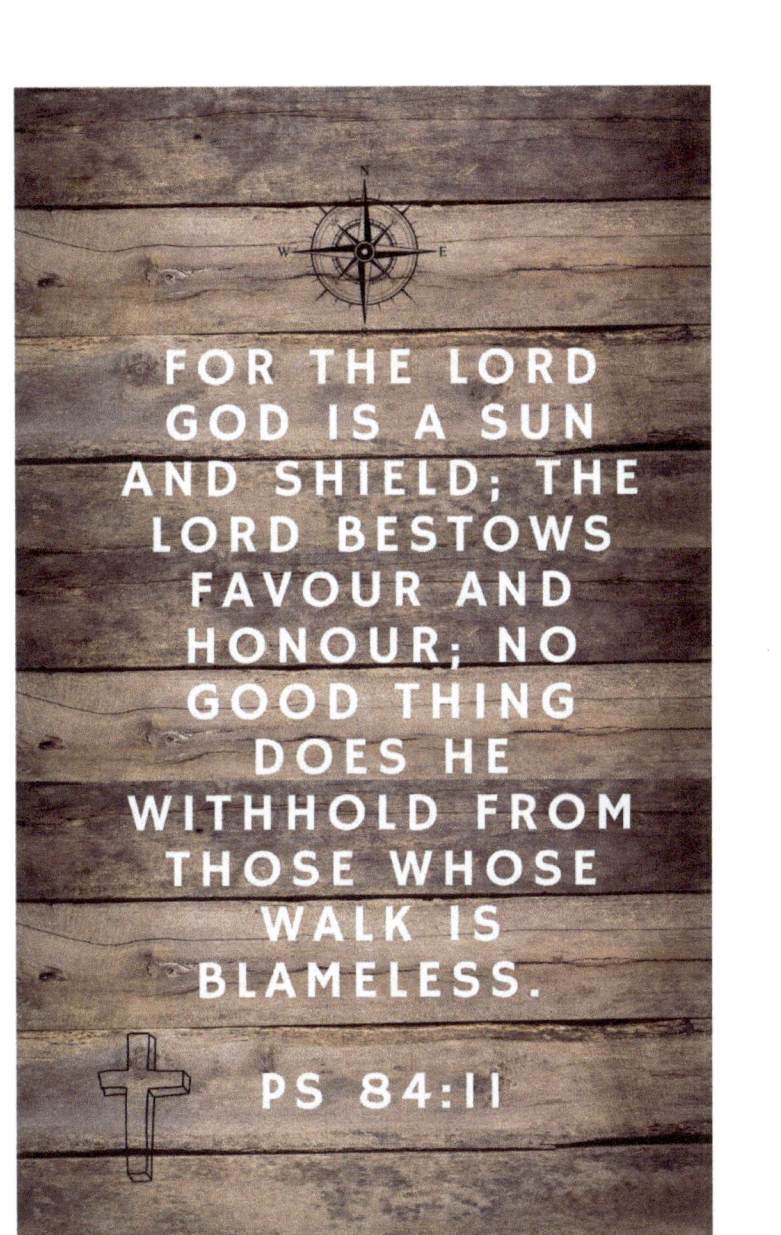

FOR THE LORD
GOD IS A SUN
AND SHIELD; THE
LORD BESTOWS
FAVOUR AND
HONOUR; NO
GOOD THING
DOES HE
WITHHOLD FROM
THOSE WHOSE
WALK IS
BLAMELESS.

PS 84:11

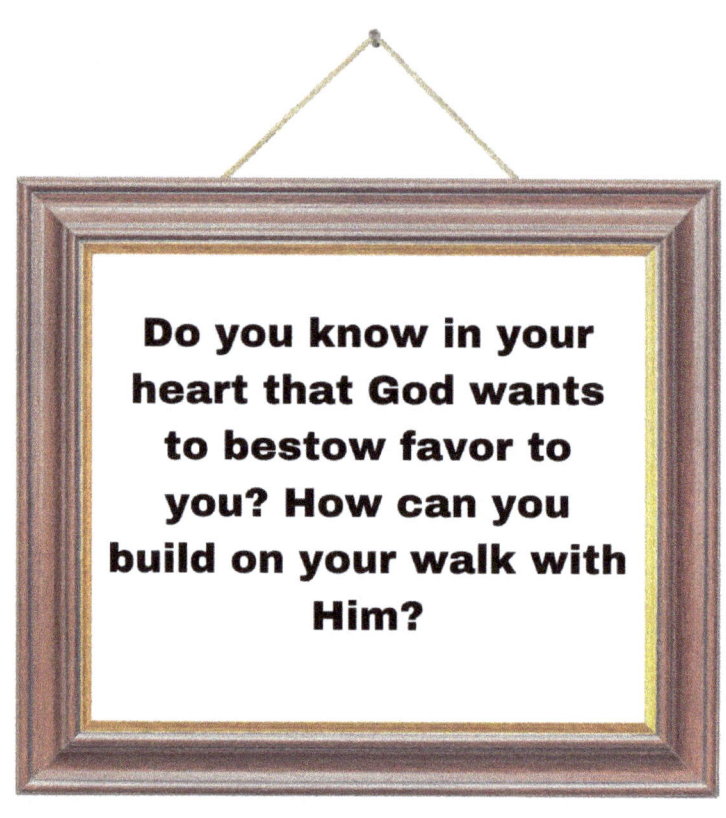

STOP...

JOURNAL TO THE LORD ABOUT WHAT THIS PROMISE MEANS TO YOU. WHY IS THIS PROMISE IMPORTANT?

ASK...

ASK THE LORD ABOUT HOW THIS PROMISE APPLIES TO YOUR LIFE RIGHT NOW. SPEAK FROM THE HEART ABOUT WHY YOU ARE ASKING.

OBEY...

HOW CAN I APPLY WHAT THE LORD HAS TOLD ME INTO MY LIFE CONSISTENTLY GOING FORWARD?

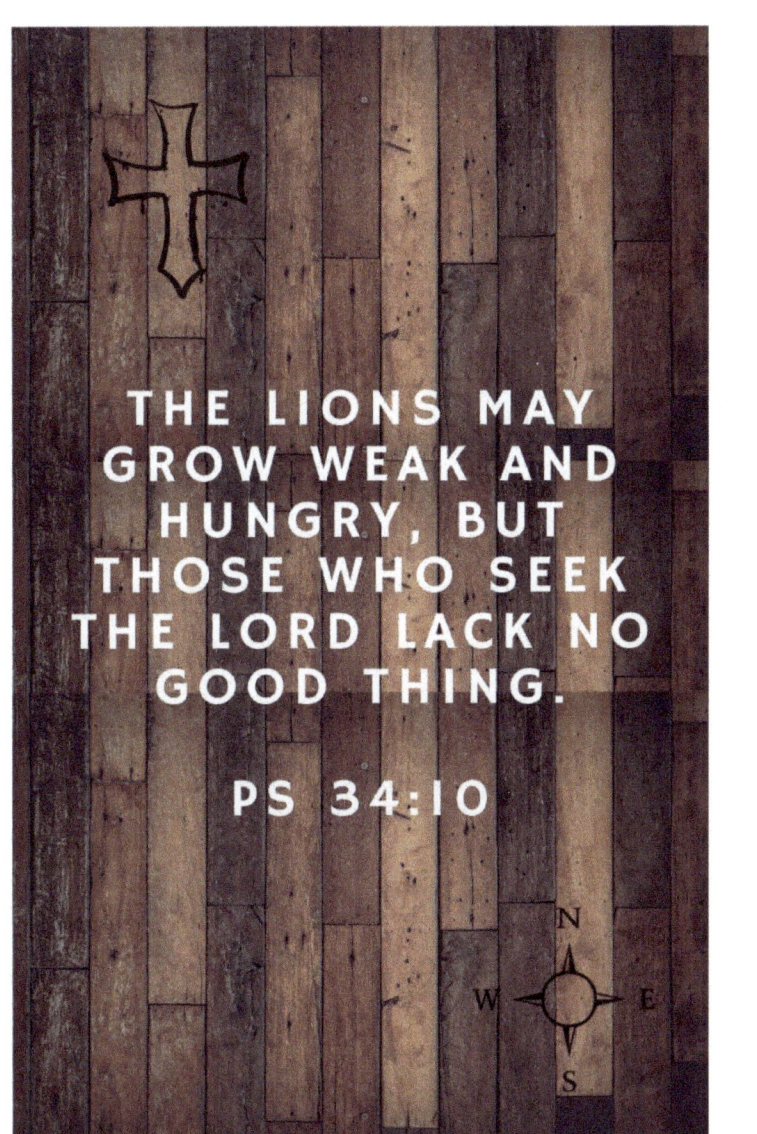

THE LIONS MAY
GROW WEAK AND
HUNGRY, BUT
THOSE WHO SEEK
THE LORD LACK NO
GOOD THING.

PS 34:10

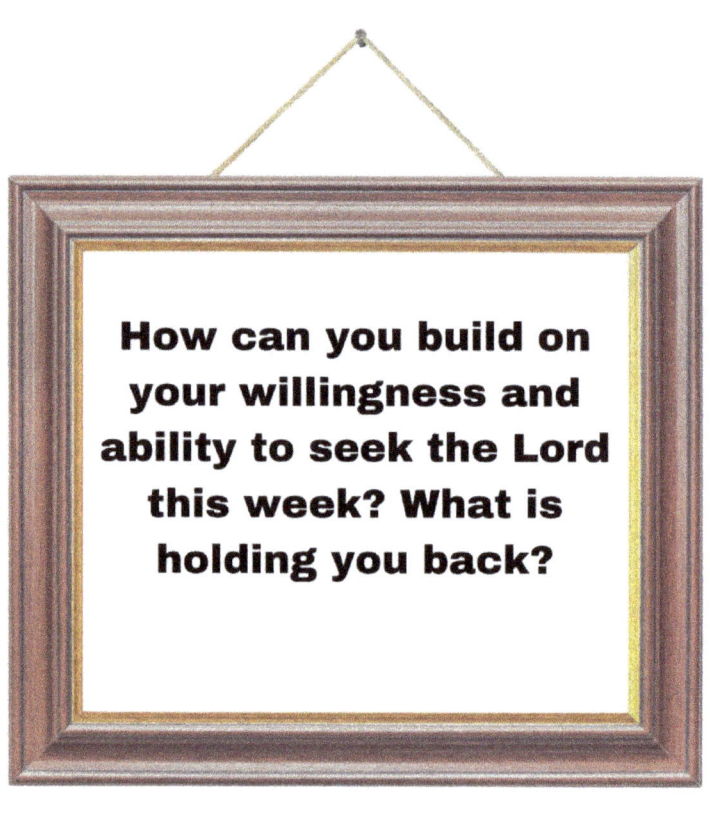

How can you build on your willingness and ability to seek the Lord this week? What is holding you back?

STOP...

JOURNAL TO THE LORD ABOUT WHAT THIS PROMISE MEANS TO YOU. WHY IS THIS PROMISE IMPORTANT?

ASK...

ASK THE LORD ABOUT HOW THIS PROMISE APPLIES TO YOUR LIFE RIGHT NOW. SPEAK FROM THE HEART ABOUT WHY YOU ARE ASKING.

OBEY...

HOW CAN I APPLY WHAT THE LORD HAS TOLD ME INTO MY LIFE CONSISTENTLY GOING FORWARD?

THE LORD HIMSELF
GOES BEFORE YOU
AND WILL BE WITH
YOU; HE WILL
NEVER LEAVE YOU
NOR FORSAKE
YOU. DO NOT BE
AFRAID; DO NOT
BE DISCOURAGED.

DEUT 31:8

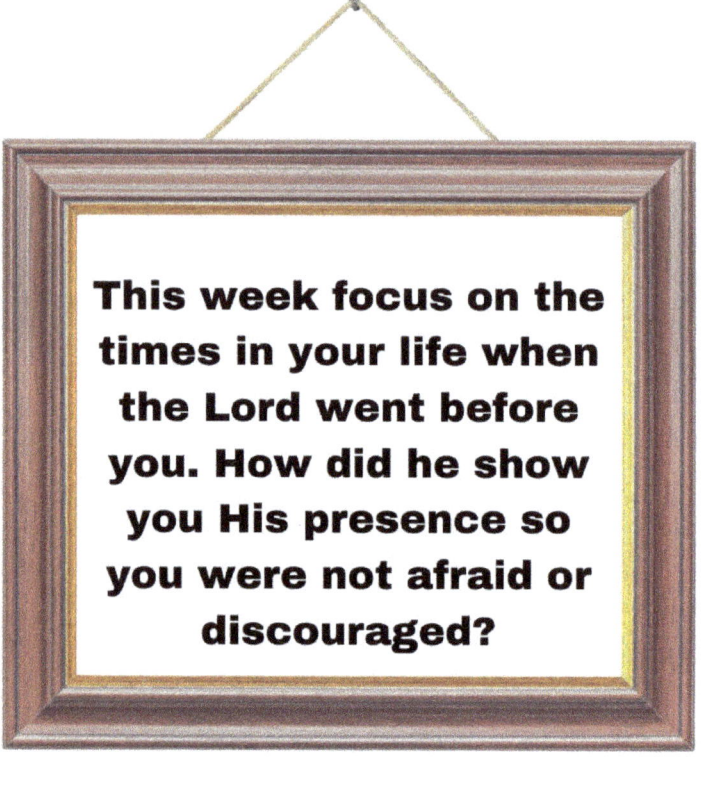

This week focus on the times in your life when the Lord went before you. How did he show you His presence so you were not afraid or discouraged?

STOP...

JOURNAL TO THE LORD ABOUT WHAT THIS PROMISE MEANS TO YOU. WHY IS THIS PROMISE IMPORTANT?

ASK...

ASK THE LORD ABOUT HOW THIS PROMISE APPLIES TO YOUR LIFE RIGHT NOW. SPEAK FROM THE HEART ABOUT WHY YOU ARE ASKING.

OBEY...

HOW CAN I APPLY WHAT THE LORD HAS TOLD ME INTO MY LIFE CONSISTENTLY GOING FORWARD?

COME TO ME, ALL
YOU WHO ARE WEARY
AND BURDENED, AND I
WILL GIVE YOU REST.
TAKE MY YOKE UPON
YOU AND LEARN FROM
ME, FOR I AM GENTLE
AND HUMBLE IN
HEART, AND YOU WILL
FIND REST FOR YOUR
SOULS. FOR MY YOKE
IS EASY AND MY
BURDEN IS LIGHT.

MATTHEW 11:28-39

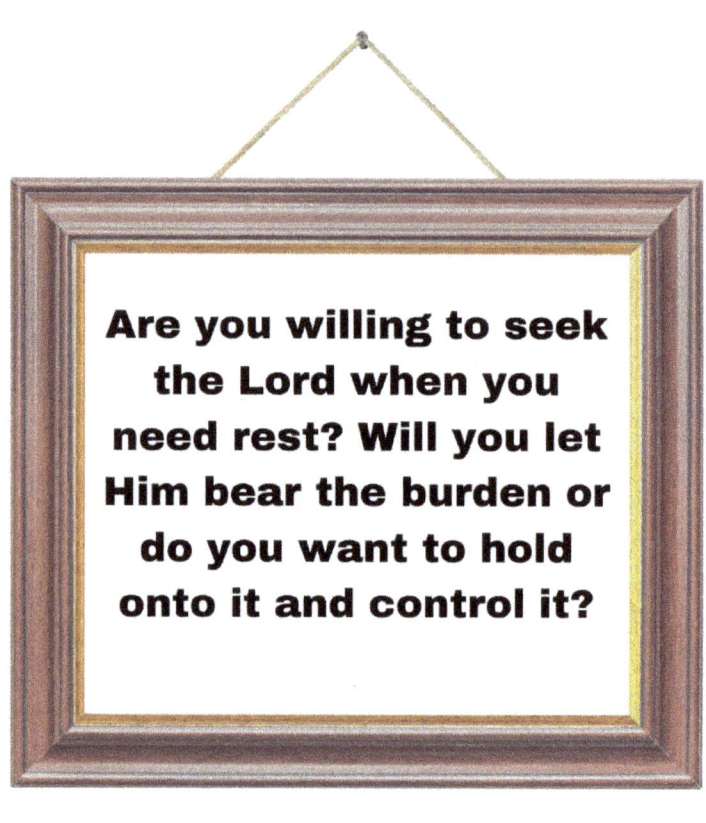

Are you willing to seek the Lord when you need rest? Will you let Him bear the burden or do you want to hold onto it and control it?

STOP...

JOURNAL TO THE LORD ABOUT WHAT THIS PROMISE MEANS TO YOU. WHY IS THIS PROMISE IMPORTANT?

ASK...

ASK THE LORD ABOUT HOW THIS PROMISE APPLIES TO YOUR LIFE RIGHT NOW. SPEAK FROM THE HEART ABOUT WHY YOU ARE ASKING.

OBEY...

HOW CAN I APPLY WHAT THE LORD HAS TOLD ME INTO MY LIFE CONSISTENTLY GOING FORWARD?

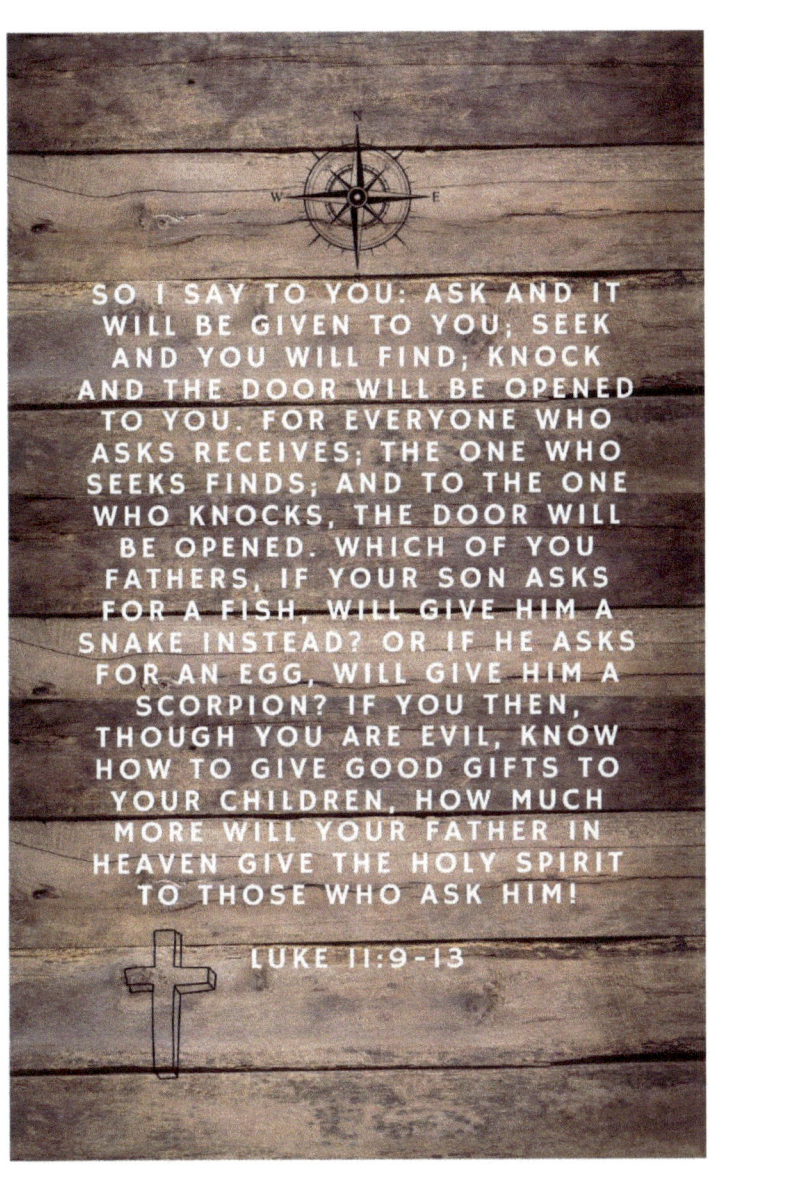

SO I SAY TO YOU: ASK AND IT WILL BE GIVEN TO YOU; SEEK AND YOU WILL FIND; KNOCK AND THE DOOR WILL BE OPENED TO YOU. FOR EVERYONE WHO ASKS RECEIVES; THE ONE WHO SEEKS FINDS; AND TO THE ONE WHO KNOCKS, THE DOOR WILL BE OPENED. WHICH OF YOU FATHERS, IF YOUR SON ASKS FOR A FISH, WILL GIVE HIM A SNAKE INSTEAD? OR IF HE ASKS FOR AN EGG, WILL GIVE HIM A SCORPION? IF YOU THEN, THOUGH YOU ARE EVIL, KNOW HOW TO GIVE GOOD GIFTS TO YOUR CHILDREN, HOW MUCH MORE WILL YOUR FATHER IN HEAVEN GIVE THE HOLY SPIRIT TO THOSE WHO ASK HIM!

LUKE 11:9-13

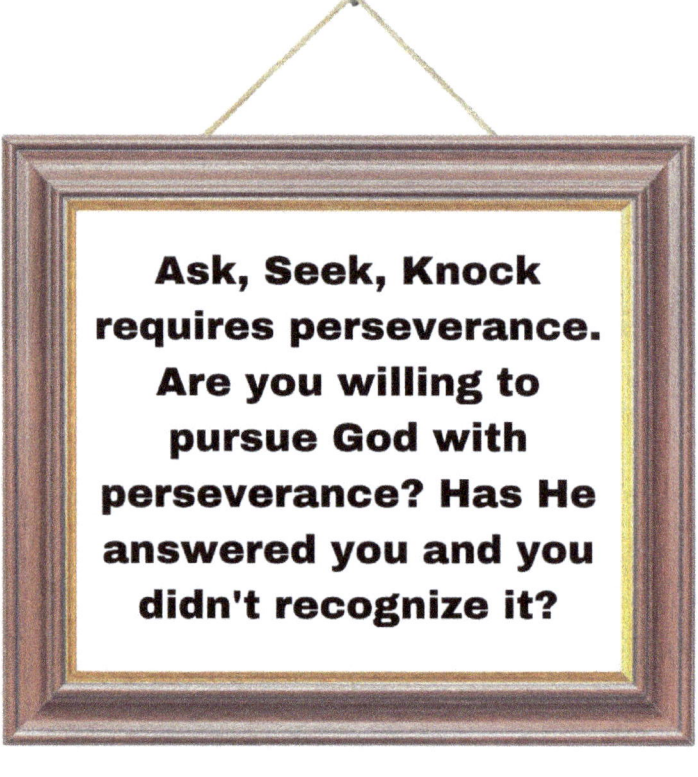

STOP...

JOURNAL TO THE LORD ABOUT WHAT THIS PROMISE MEANS TO YOU. WHY IS THIS PROMISE IMPORTANT?

ASK...

ASK THE LORD ABOUT HOW THIS PROMISE APPLIES TO YOUR LIFE RIGHT NOW. SPEAK FROM THE HEART ABOUT WHY YOU ARE ASKING.

OBEY...

HOW CAN I APPLY WHAT THE LORD HAS TOLD ME INTO MY LIFE CONSISTENTLY GOING FORWARD?

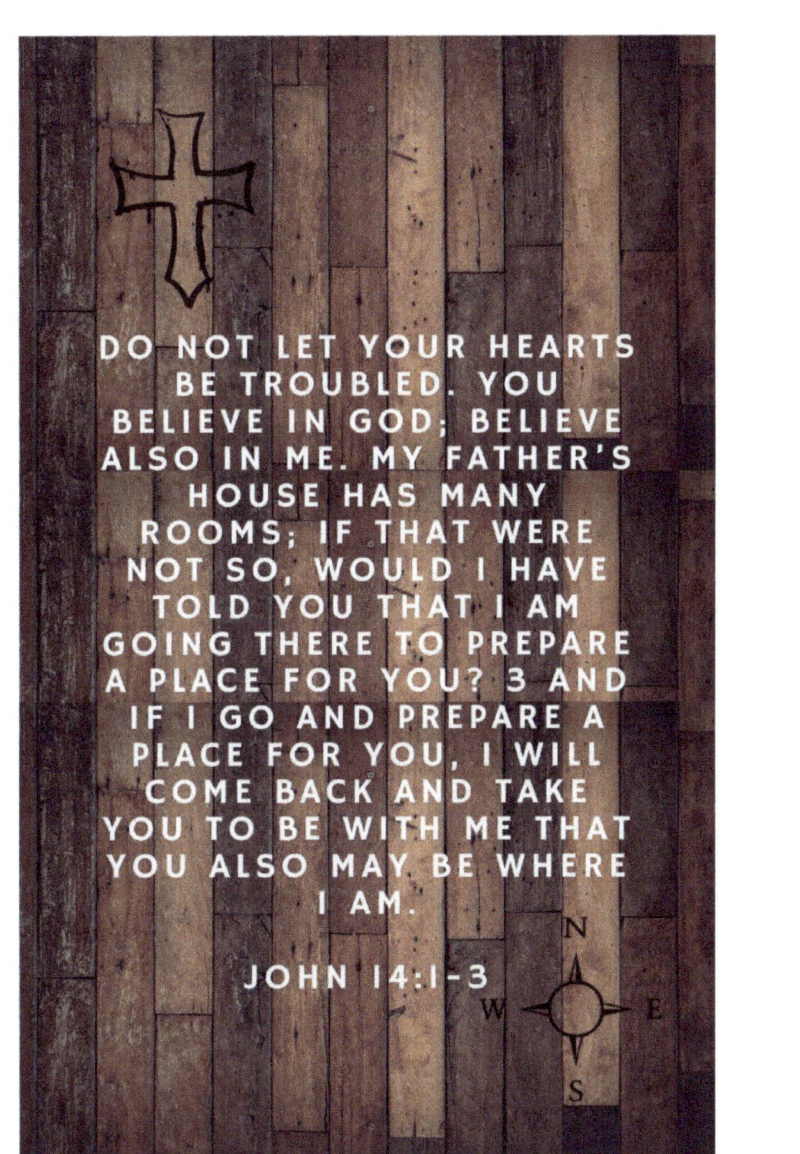

DO NOT LET YOUR HEARTS
BE TROUBLED. YOU
BELIEVE IN GOD; BELIEVE
ALSO IN ME. MY FATHER'S
HOUSE HAS MANY
ROOMS; IF THAT WERE
NOT SO, WOULD I HAVE
TOLD YOU THAT I AM
GOING THERE TO PREPARE
A PLACE FOR YOU? 3 AND
IF I GO AND PREPARE A
PLACE FOR YOU, I WILL
COME BACK AND TAKE
YOU TO BE WITH ME THAT
YOU ALSO MAY BE WHERE
I AM.

JOHN 14:1-3

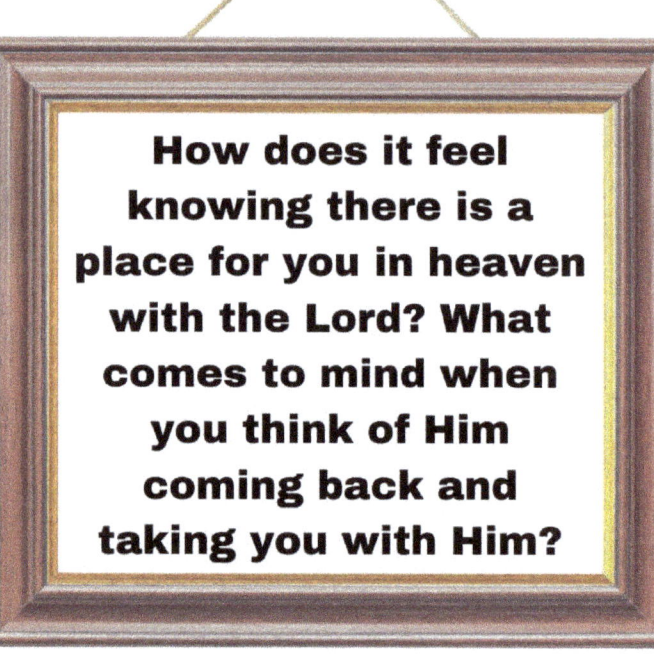

STOP...

JOURNAL TO THE LORD ABOUT WHAT THIS PROMISE MEANS TO YOU. WHY IS THIS PROMISE IMPORTANT?

ASK...

ASK THE LORD ABOUT HOW THIS PROMISE APPLIES TO YOUR LIFE RIGHT NOW. SPEAK FROM THE HEART ABOUT WHY YOU ARE ASKING.

OBEY...

HOW CAN I APPLY WHAT THE LORD HAS TOLD ME INTO MY LIFE CONSISTENTLY GOING FORWARD?

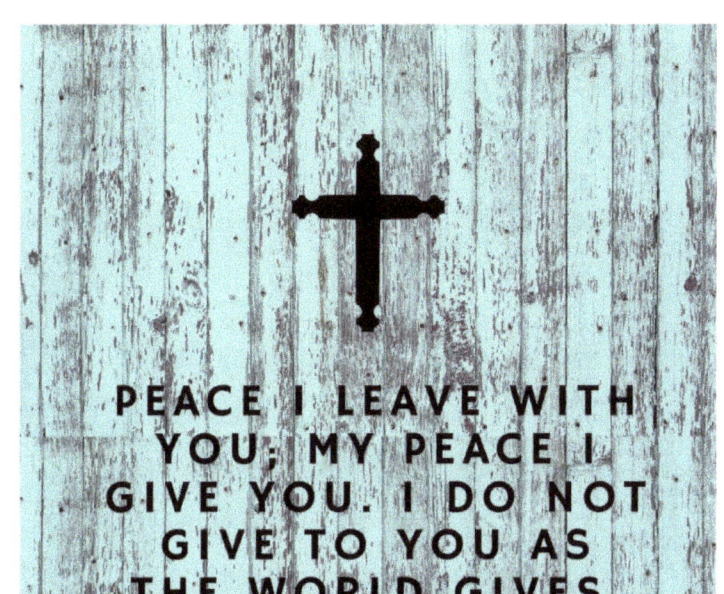

PEACE I LEAVE WITH
YOU; MY PEACE I
GIVE YOU. I DO NOT
GIVE TO YOU AS
THE WORLD GIVES.
DO NOT LET YOUR
HEARTS BE
TROUBLED AND DO
NOT BE AFRAID.

JOHN 14:27

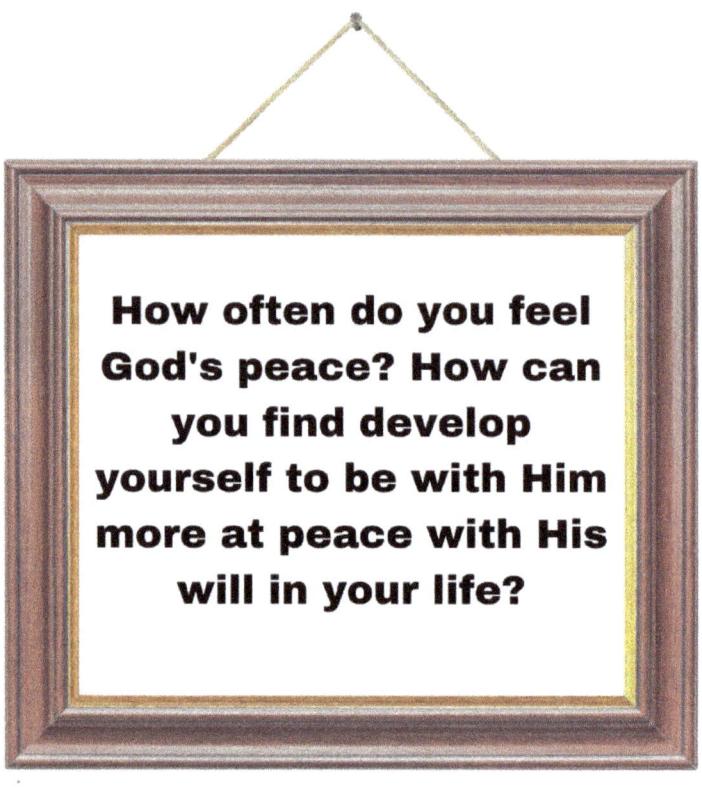

How often do you feel God's peace? How can you find develop yourself to be with Him more at peace with His will in your life?

STOP...

JOURNAL TO THE LORD ABOUT WHAT THIS PROMISE MEANS TO YOU. WHY IS THIS PROMISE IMPORTANT?

ASK...

ASK THE LORD ABOUT HOW THIS PROMISE APPLIES TO YOUR LIFE RIGHT NOW. SPEAK FROM THE HEART ABOUT WHY YOU ARE ASKING.

OBEY...

HOW CAN I APPLY WHAT THE LORD HAS TOLD ME INTO MY LIFE CONSISTENTLY GOING FORWARD?

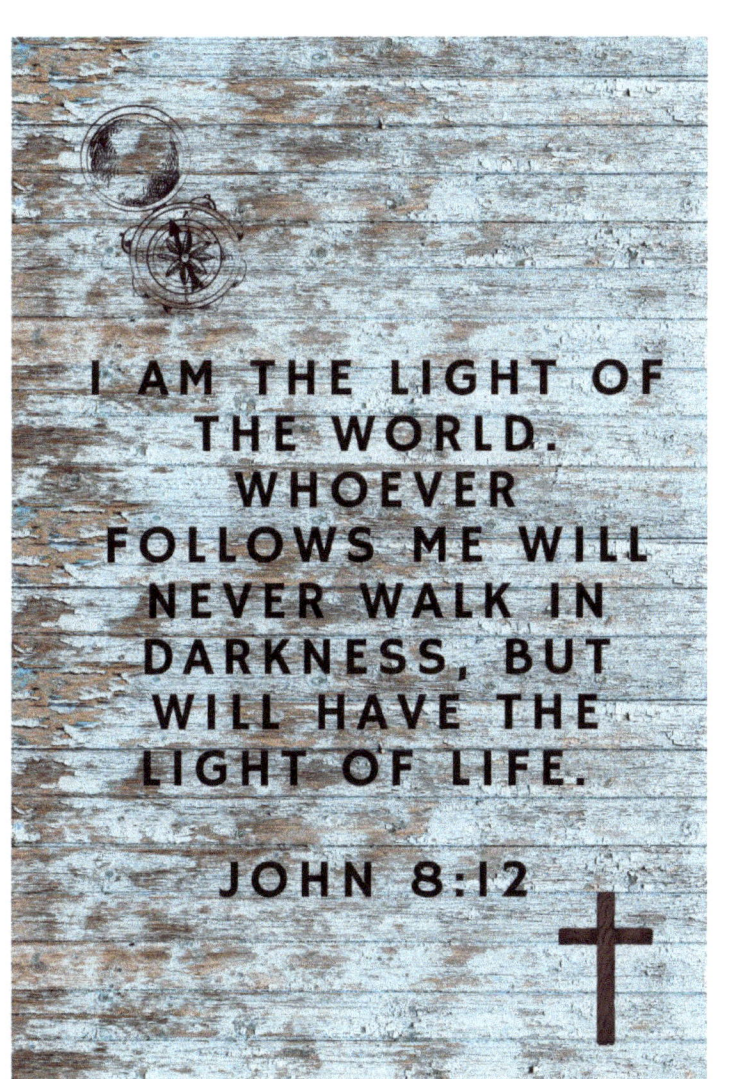

I AM THE LIGHT OF THE WORLD. WHOEVER FOLLOWS ME WILL NEVER WALK IN DARKNESS, BUT WILL HAVE THE LIGHT OF LIFE.

JOHN 8:12

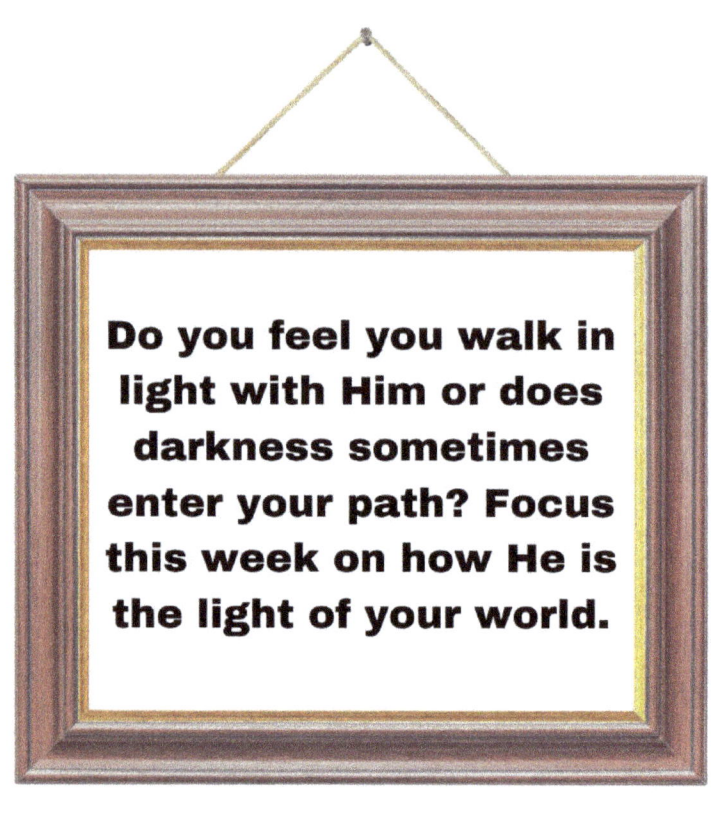

Do you feel you walk in light with Him or does darkness sometimes enter your path? Focus this week on how He is the light of your world.

STOP...

JOURNAL TO THE LORD ABOUT WHAT THIS PROMISE MEANS TO YOU. WHY IS THIS PROMISE IMPORTANT?

ASK...

ASK THE LORD ABOUT HOW THIS PROMISE APPLIES TO YOUR LIFE RIGHT NOW. SPEAK FROM THE HEART ABOUT WHY YOU ARE ASKING.

OBEY...

HOW CAN I APPLY WHAT THE LORD HAS TOLD ME INTO MY LIFE CONSISTENTLY GOING FORWARD?

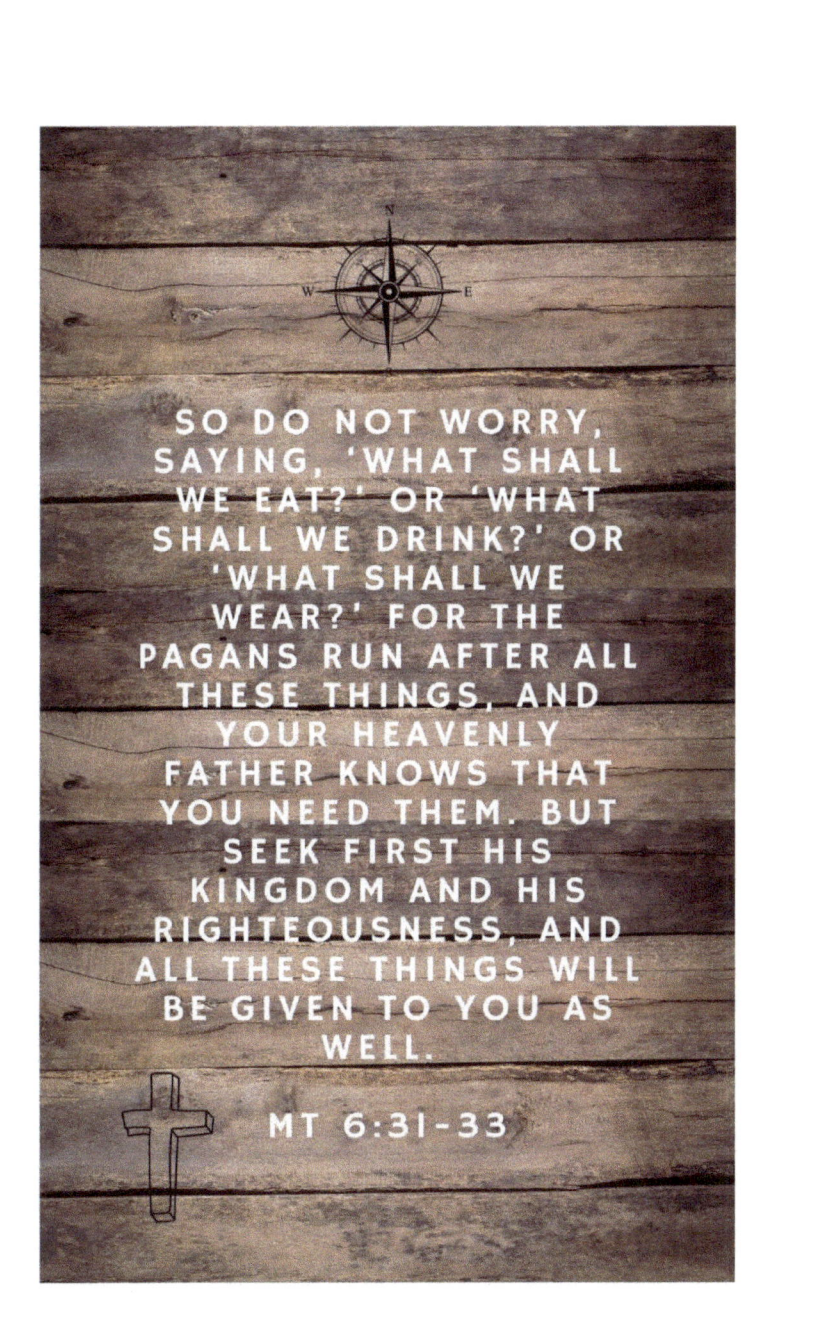

SO DO NOT WORRY, SAYING, 'WHAT SHALL WE EAT?' OR 'WHAT SHALL WE DRINK?' OR 'WHAT SHALL WE WEAR?' FOR THE PAGANS RUN AFTER ALL THESE THINGS, AND YOUR HEAVENLY FATHER KNOWS THAT YOU NEED THEM. BUT SEEK FIRST HIS KINGDOM AND HIS RIGHTEOUSNESS, AND ALL THESE THINGS WILL BE GIVEN TO YOU AS WELL.

MT 6:31-33

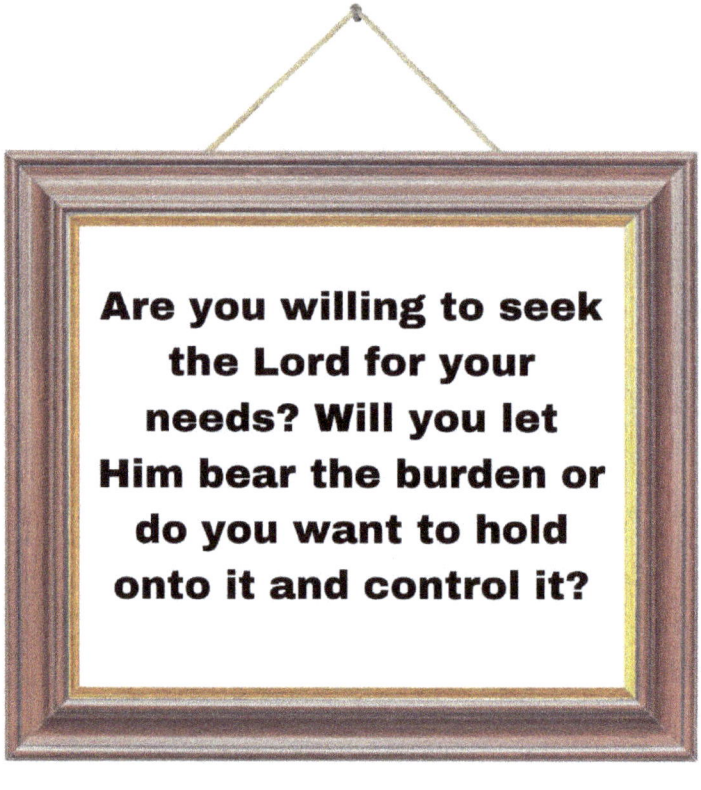

Are you willing to seek the Lord for your needs? Will you let Him bear the burden or do you want to hold onto it and control it?

STOP...

JOURNAL TO THE LORD ABOUT WHAT THIS PROMISE MEANS TO YOU. WHY IS THIS PROMISE IMPORTANT?

ASK...

ASK THE LORD ABOUT HOW THIS PROMISE APPLIES TO YOUR LIFE RIGHT NOW. SPEAK FROM THE HEART ABOUT WHY YOU ARE ASKING.

LISTEN...

LORD, TELL ME WHAT YOU HAVE TO SAY ABOUT HOW YOUR PROMISE APPLIES TO ME.

OBEY...

HOW CAN I APPLY WHAT THE LORD HAS TOLD ME INTO MY LIFE CONSISTENTLY GOING FORWARD?

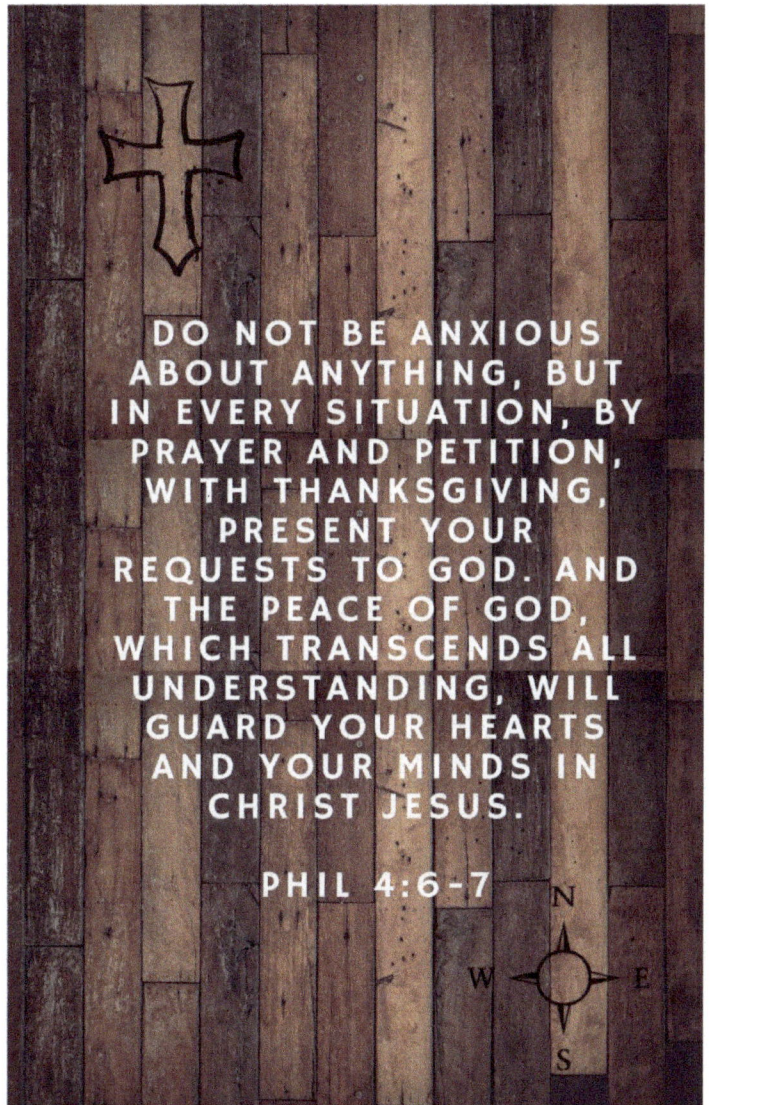

DO NOT BE ANXIOUS ABOUT ANYTHING, BUT IN EVERY SITUATION, BY PRAYER AND PETITION, WITH THANKSGIVING, PRESENT YOUR REQUESTS TO GOD. AND THE PEACE OF GOD, WHICH TRANSCENDS ALL UNDERSTANDING, WILL GUARD YOUR HEARTS AND YOUR MINDS IN CHRIST JESUS.

PHIL 4:6-7

Do you spend time worrying before you present your requests to God? How can you redirect your focus to thanksgiving even in hard times?

STOP...

JOURNAL TO THE LORD ABOUT WHAT THIS PROMISE MEANS TO YOU. WHY IS THIS PROMISE IMPORTANT?

ASK...

ASK THE LORD ABOUT HOW THIS PROMISE APPLIES TO YOUR LIFE RIGHT NOW. SPEAK FROM THE HEART ABOUT WHY YOU ARE ASKING.

OBEY...

HOW CAN I APPLY WHAT THE LORD HAS TOLD ME INTO MY LIFE CONSISTENTLY GOING FORWARD?

EVERY GOOD AND
PERFECT GIFT IS
FROM ABOVE, COMING
DOWN FROM THE
FATHER OF THE
HEAVENLY LIGHTS,
WHO DOES NOT
CHANGE LIKE
SHIFTING SHADOWS.

JAMES 1:17

Do you believe that what God gives you are good and perfect gifts? Do you now in your heart He is the same yesterday, today and tomorrow?

STOP...

JOURNAL TO THE LORD ABOUT WHAT THIS PROMISE MEANS TO YOU. WHY IS THIS PROMISE IMPORTANT?

ASK...

ASK THE LORD ABOUT HOW THIS PROMISE APPLIES TO YOUR LIFE RIGHT NOW. SPEAK FROM THE HEART ABOUT WHY YOU ARE ASKING.

OBEY...

HOW CAN I APPLY WHAT THE LORD HAS TOLD ME INTO MY LIFE CONSISTENTLY GOING FORWARD?

SOVEREIGN LORD,
YOU ARE GOD!
YOUR COVENANT
IS TRUSTWORTHY,
AND YOU HAVE
PROMISED THESE
GOOD THINGS TO
YOUR SERVANT. . .

2 SAM 7:28

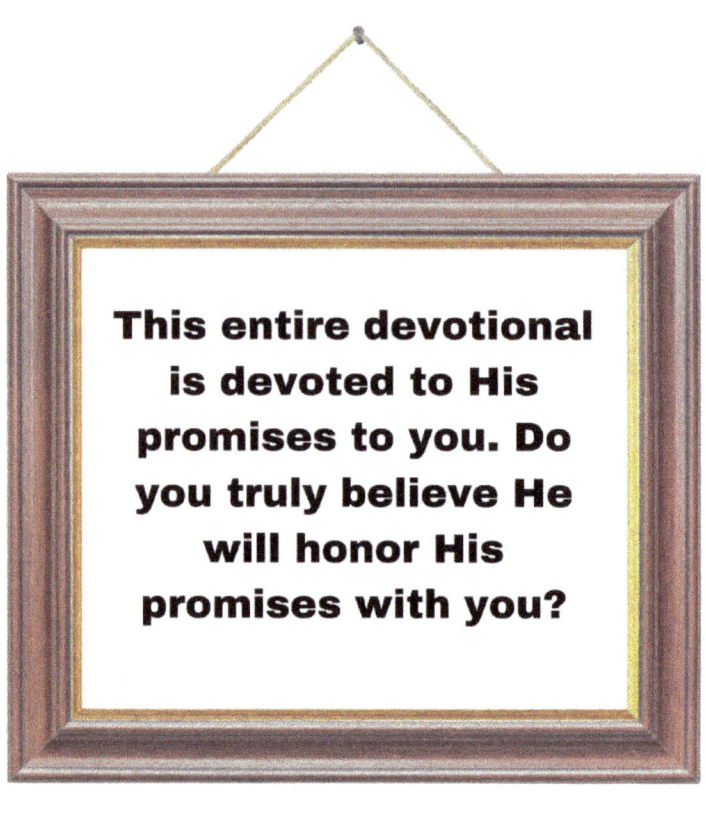

STOP...

JOURNAL TO THE LORD ABOUT WHAT THIS PROMISE MEANS TO YOU. WHY IS THIS PROMISE IMPORTANT?

ASK...

ASK THE LORD ABOUT HOW THIS PROMISE APPLIES TO YOUR LIFE RIGHT NOW. SPEAK FROM THE HEART ABOUT WHY YOU ARE ASKING.

OBEY...

HOW CAN I APPLY WHAT THE LORD HAS TOLD ME INTO MY LIFE CONSISTENTLY GOING FORWARD?

THE LORD IS GOOD, A REFUGE IN TIMES OF TROUBLE. HE CARES FOR THOSE WHO TRUST IN HIM.

NAHUM 1:7

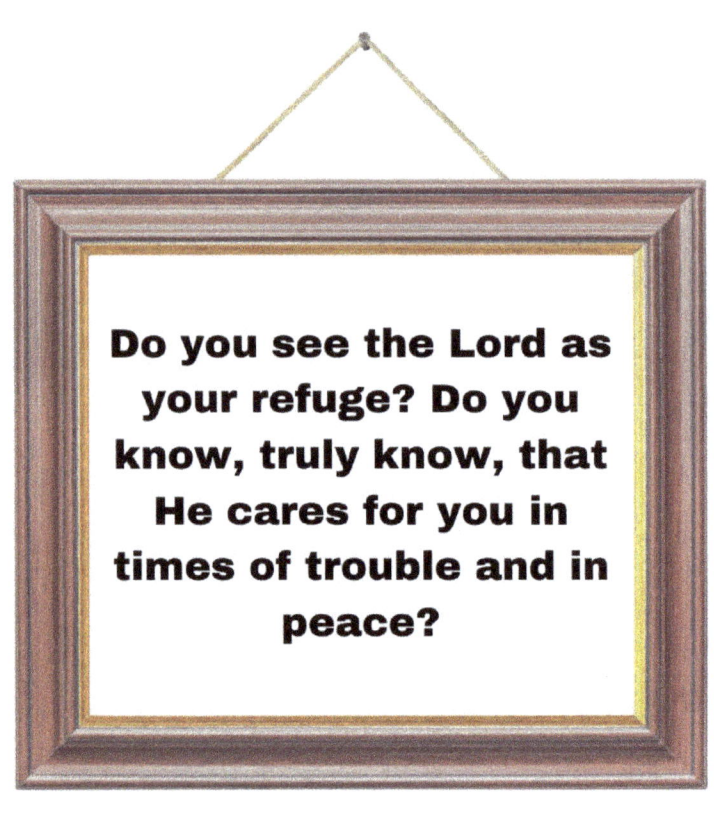

Do you see the Lord as your refuge? Do you know, truly know, that He cares for you in times of trouble and in peace?

STOP...

JOURNAL TO THE LORD ABOUT WHAT THIS PROMISE MEANS TO YOU. WHY IS THIS PROMISE IMPORTANT?

ASK...

ASK THE LORD ABOUT HOW THIS PROMISE APPLIES TO YOUR LIFE RIGHT NOW. SPEAK FROM THE HEART ABOUT WHY YOU ARE ASKING.

OBEY...

HOW CAN I APPLY WHAT THE LORD HAS TOLD ME INTO MY LIFE CONSISTENTLY GOING FORWARD?

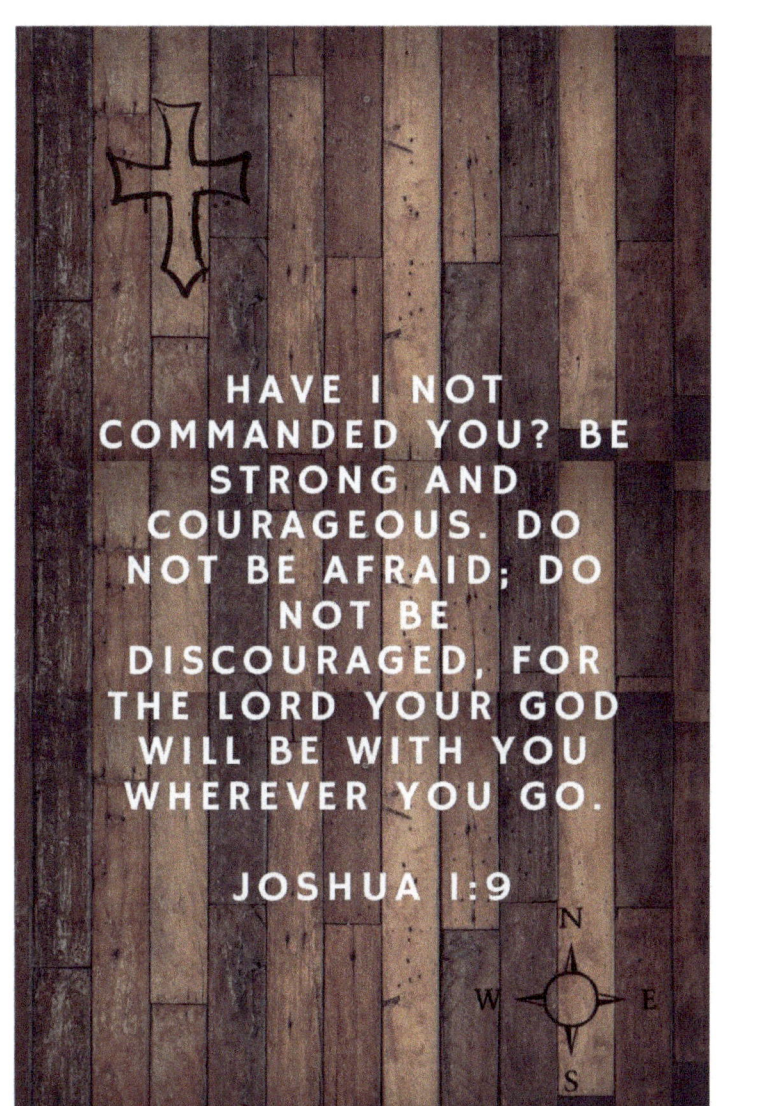

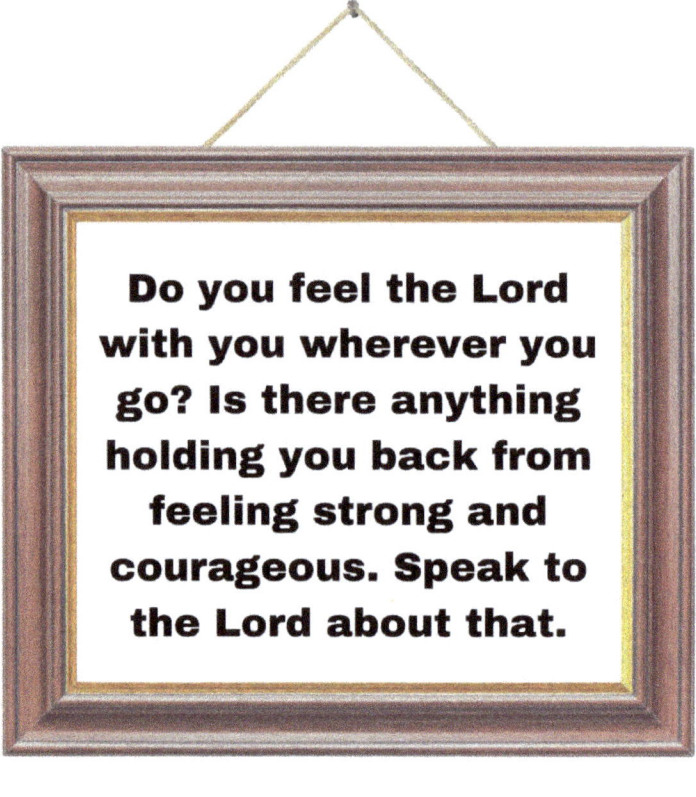

Do you feel the Lord with you wherever you go? Is there anything holding you back from feeling strong and courageous. Speak to the Lord about that.

STOP...

JOURNAL TO THE LORD ABOUT WHAT THIS PROMISE MEANS TO YOU. WHY IS THIS PROMISE IMPORTANT?

ASK...

ASK THE LORD ABOUT HOW THIS PROMISE APPLIES TO YOUR LIFE RIGHT NOW. SPEAK FROM THE HEART ABOUT WHY YOU ARE ASKING.

OBEY...

HOW CAN I APPLY WHAT THE LORD HAS TOLD ME INTO MY LIFE CONSISTENTLY GOING FORWARD?

YES, I AM THE VINE;
YOU ARE THE
BRANCHES. THOSE
WHO REMAIN IN ME,
AND I IN THEM, WILL
PRODUCE MUCH
FRUIT. FOR APART
FROM ME YOU CAN
DO NOTHING.

JOHN 15:5

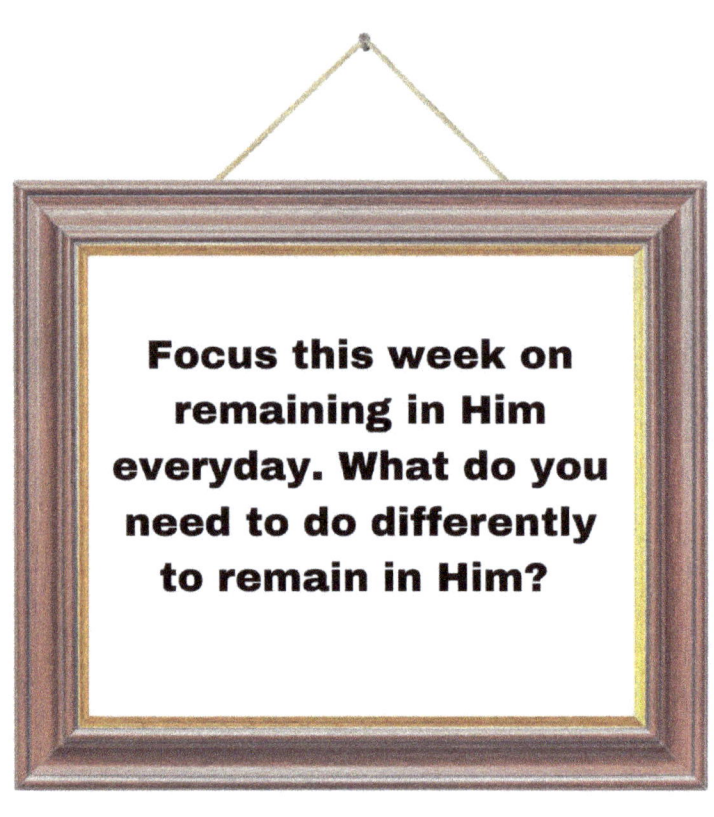

STOP...

JOURNAL TO THE LORD ABOUT WHAT THIS PROMISE MEANS TO YOU. WHY IS THIS PROMISE IMPORTANT?

ASK...

ASK THE LORD ABOUT HOW THIS PROMISE APPLIES TO YOUR LIFE RIGHT NOW. SPEAK FROM THE HEART ABOUT WHY YOU ARE ASKING.

OBEY...

HOW CAN I APPLY WHAT THE LORD HAS TOLD ME INTO MY LIFE CONSISTENTLY GOING FORWARD?

BLESSED IS THE ONE
WHO DOES NOT WALK IN STEP
WITH THE WICKED
OR STAND IN THE WAY THAT
SINNERS TAKE
OR SIT IN THE COMPANY OF
MOCKERS,
BUT WHOSE DELIGHT IS IN THE
LAW OF THE LORD,
AND WHO MEDITATES ON HIS
LAW DAY AND NIGHT.
THAT PERSON IS LIKE A TREE
PLANTED BY STREAMS OF WATER,
WHICH YIELDS ITS FRUIT IN
SEASON
AND WHOSE LEAF DOES NOT
WITHER—
WHATEVER THEY DO PROSPERS.

PSALM 1:1-3

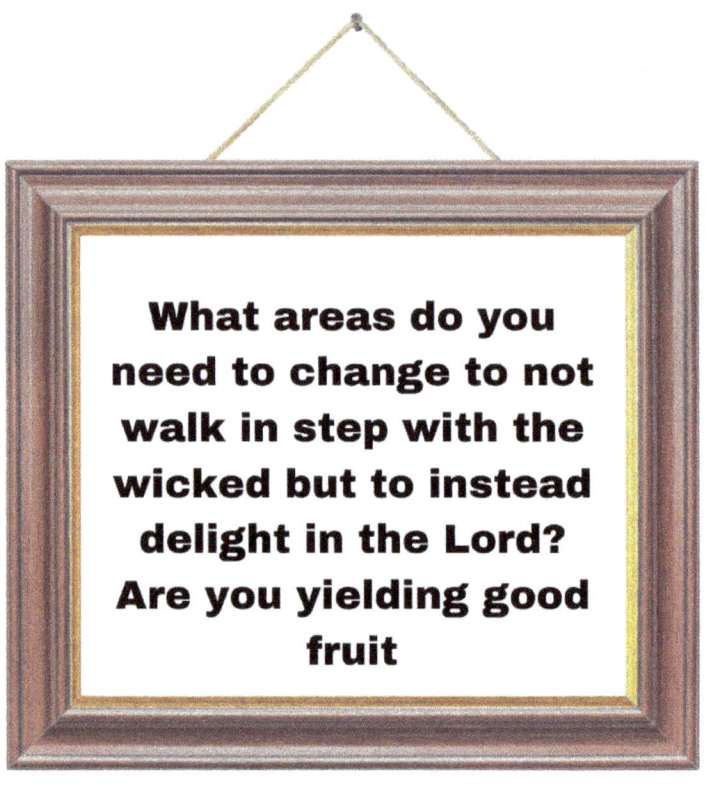

What areas do you need to change to not walk in step with the wicked but to instead delight in the Lord? Are you yielding good fruit

STOP...

JOURNAL TO THE LORD ABOUT WHAT THIS PROMISE MEANS TO YOU. WHY IS THIS PROMISE IMPORTANT?

ASK...

ASK THE LORD ABOUT HOW THIS PROMISE APPLIES TO YOUR LIFE RIGHT NOW. SPEAK FROM THE HEART ABOUT WHY YOU ARE ASKING.

OBEY...

HOW CAN I APPLY WHAT THE LORD HAS TOLD ME INTO MY LIFE CONSISTENTLY GOING FORWARD?

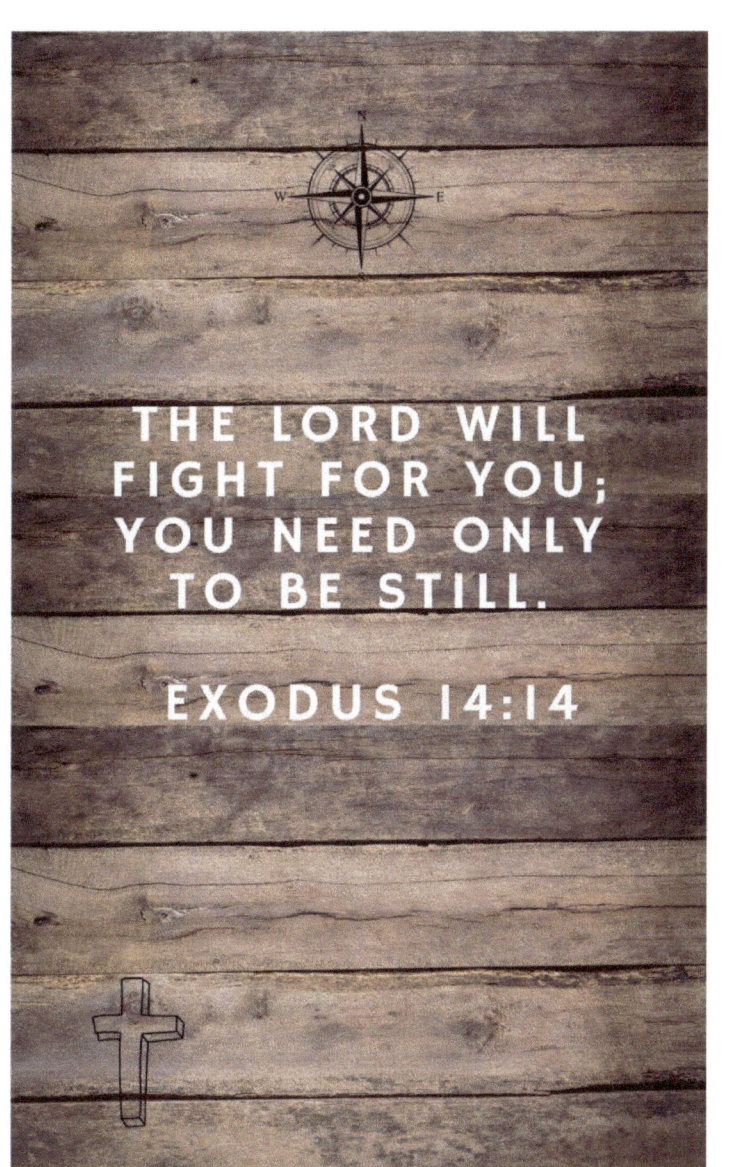

THE LORD WILL
FIGHT FOR YOU;
YOU NEED ONLY
TO BE STILL.

EXODUS 14:14

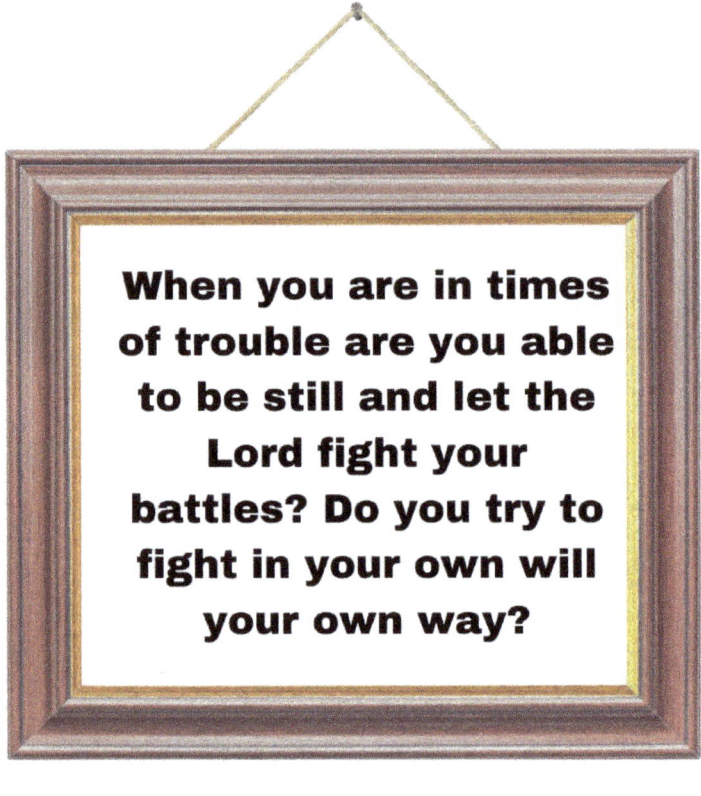

STOP...

JOURNAL TO THE LORD ABOUT WHAT THIS PROMISE MEANS TO YOU. WHY IS THIS PROMISE IMPORTANT?

ASK...

ASK THE LORD ABOUT HOW THIS PROMISE APPLIES TO YOUR LIFE RIGHT NOW. SPEAK FROM THE HEART ABOUT WHY YOU ARE ASKING.

LISTEN...

LORD, TELL ME WHAT YOU HAVE TO SAY ABOUT HOW YOUR PROMISE APPLIES TO ME.

OBEY...

HOW CAN I APPLY WHAT THE LORD HAS TOLD ME INTO MY LIFE CONSISTENTLY GOING FORWARD?

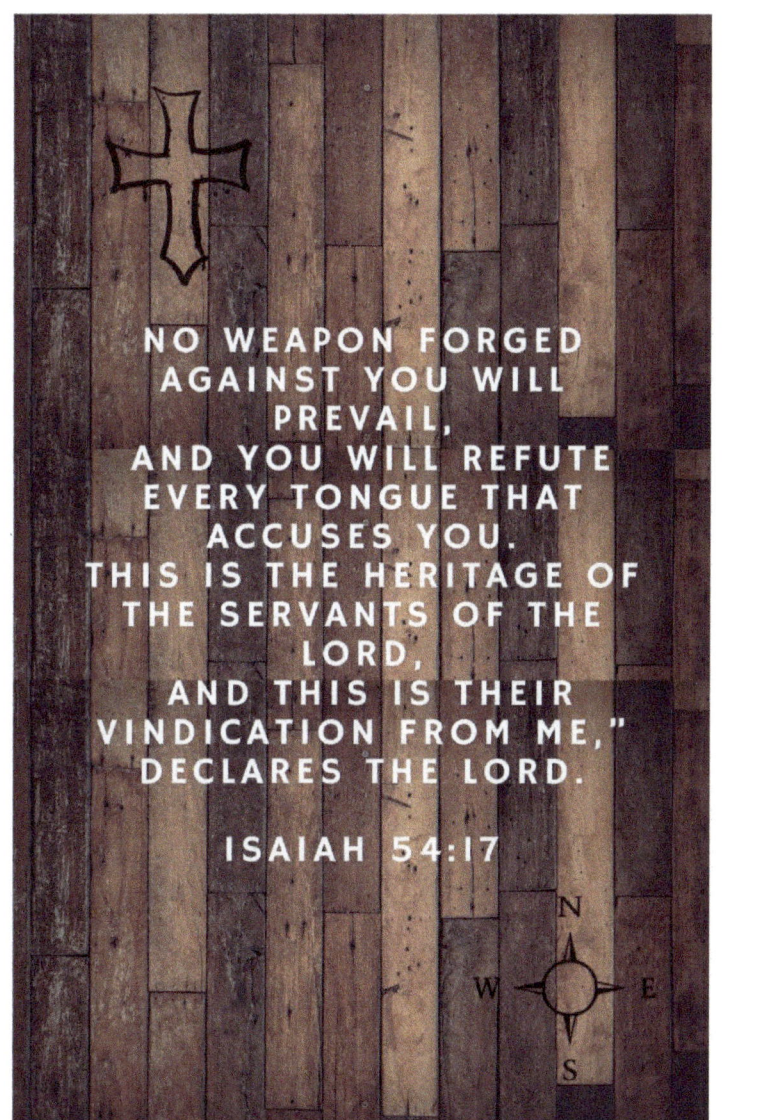

NO WEAPON FORGED
AGAINST YOU WILL
PREVAIL,
AND YOU WILL REFUTE
EVERY TONGUE THAT
ACCUSES YOU.
THIS IS THE HERITAGE OF
THE SERVANTS OF THE
LORD,
AND THIS IS THEIR
VINDICATION FROM ME,"
DECLARES THE LORD.

ISAIAH 54:17

Think this week about
weapons that have
been directed at you
and accusations made
against you. Did you
seek God in those
times? How did He
prevail on your behalf?

STOP...

JOURNAL TO THE LORD ABOUT WHAT THIS PROMISE MEANS TO YOU. WHY IS THIS PROMISE IMPORTANT?

ASK...

ASK THE LORD ABOUT HOW THIS PROMISE APPLIES TO YOUR LIFE RIGHT NOW. SPEAK FROM THE HEART ABOUT WHY YOU ARE ASKING.

OBEY...

HOW CAN I APPLY WHAT THE LORD HAS TOLD ME INTO MY LIFE CONSISTENTLY GOING FORWARD?

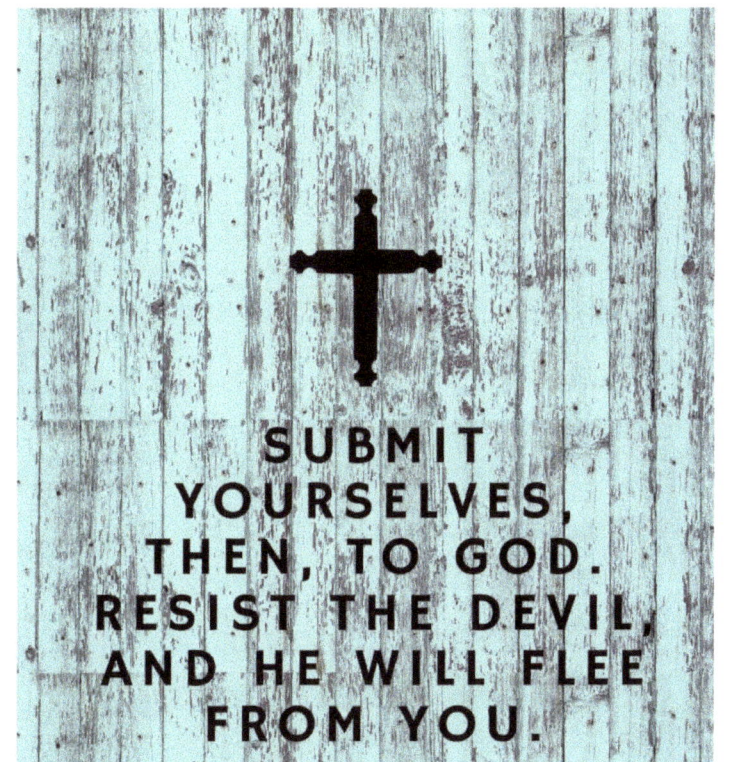

SUBMIT
YOURSELVES,
THEN, TO GOD.
RESIST THE DEVIL,
AND HE WILL FLEE
FROM YOU.

JAMES 4:7

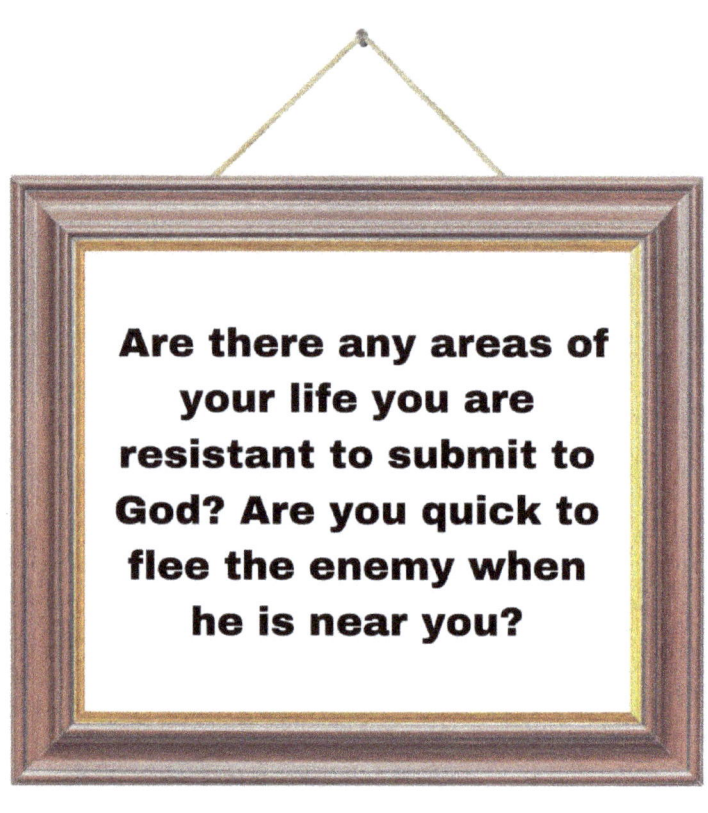

Are there any areas of your life you are resistant to submit to God? Are you quick to flee the enemy when he is near you?

STOP...

JOURNAL TO THE LORD ABOUT WHAT THIS PROMISE MEANS TO YOU. WHY IS THIS PROMISE IMPORTANT?

ASK...

ASK THE LORD ABOUT HOW THIS PROMISE APPLIES TO YOUR LIFE RIGHT NOW. SPEAK FROM THE HEART ABOUT WHY YOU ARE ASKING.

OBEY...

HOW CAN I APPLY WHAT THE LORD HAS TOLD ME INTO MY LIFE CONSISTENTLY GOING FORWARD?

BRING THE WHOLE TITHE
INTO THE STOREHOUSE,
THAT THERE MAY BE
FOOD IN MY HOUSE.
TEST ME IN THIS," SAYS
THE LORD ALMIGHTY,
"AND SEE IF I WILL NOT
THROW OPEN THE
FLOODGATES OF HEAVEN
AND POUR OUT SO MUCH
BLESSING THAT THERE
WILL NOT BE ROOM
ENOUGH TO STORE IT.

MALACHI 3:10

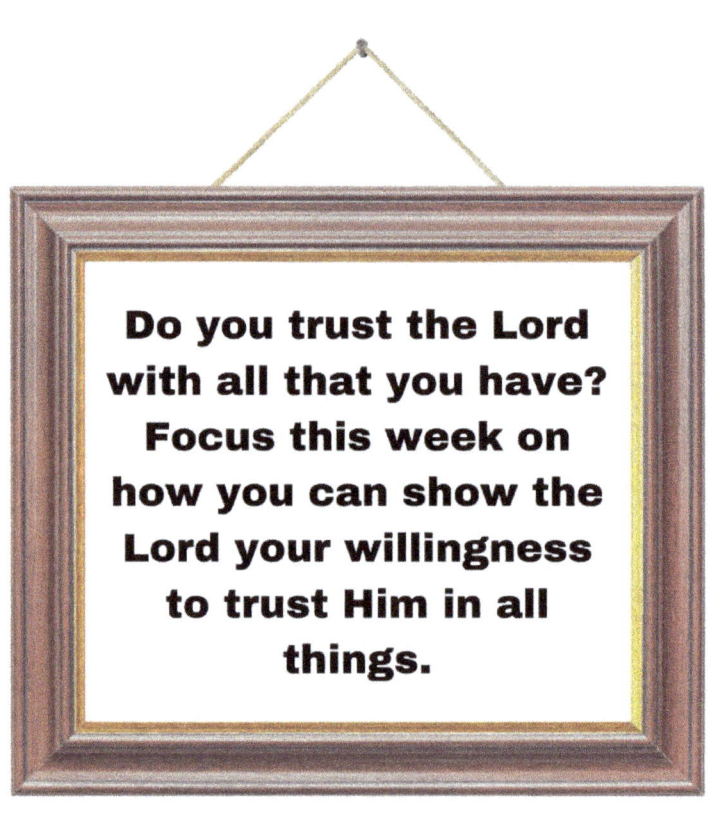

STOP...

JOURNAL TO THE LORD ABOUT WHAT THIS PROMISE MEANS TO YOU. WHY IS THIS PROMISE IMPORTANT?

ASK...

ASK THE LORD ABOUT HOW THIS PROMISE APPLIES TO YOUR LIFE RIGHT NOW. SPEAK FROM THE HEART ABOUT WHY YOU ARE ASKING.

OBEY...

HOW CAN I APPLY WHAT THE LORD HAS TOLD ME INTO MY LIFE CONSISTENTLY GOING FORWARD?

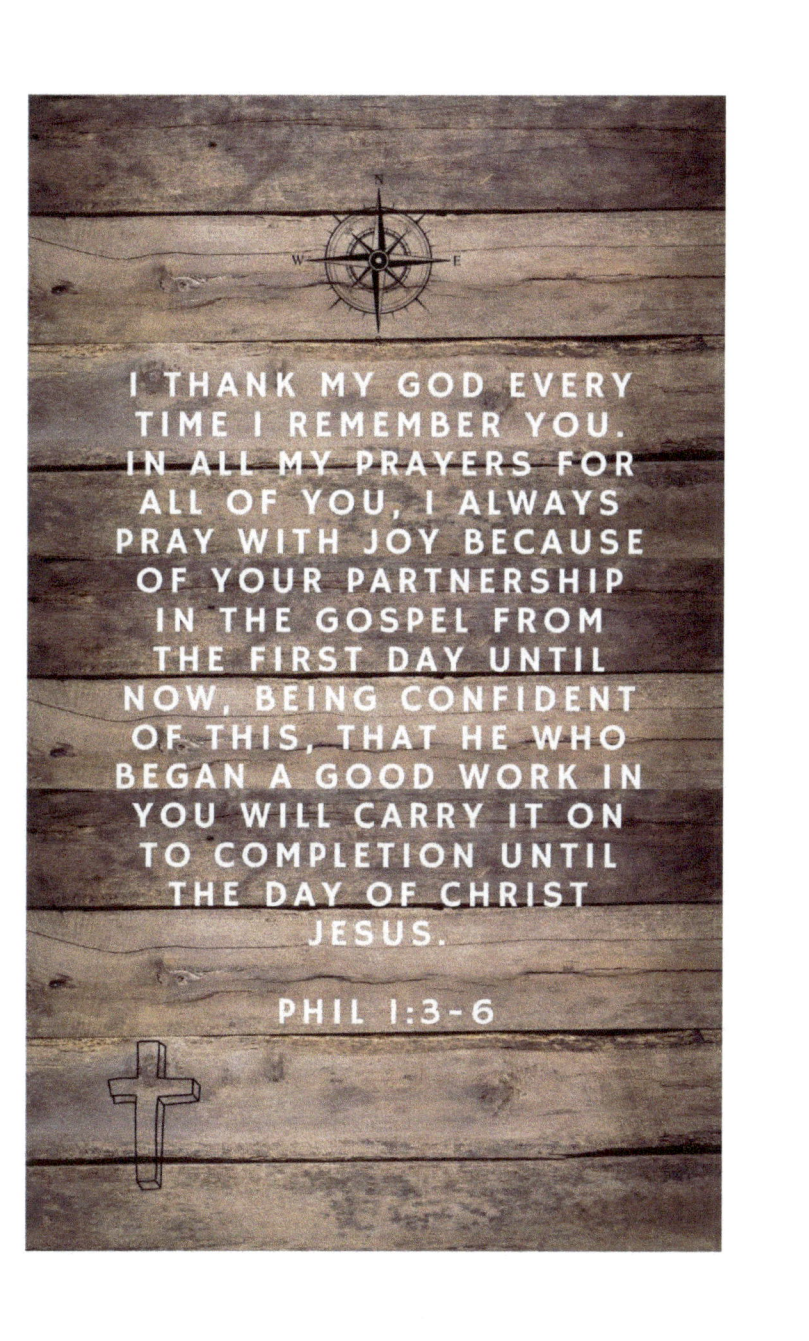

I THANK MY GOD EVERY
TIME I REMEMBER YOU.
IN ALL MY PRAYERS FOR
ALL OF YOU, I ALWAYS
PRAY WITH JOY BECAUSE
OF YOUR PARTNERSHIP
IN THE GOSPEL FROM
THE FIRST DAY UNTIL
NOW, BEING CONFIDENT
OF THIS, THAT HE WHO
BEGAN A GOOD WORK IN
YOU WILL CARRY IT ON
TO COMPLETION UNTIL
THE DAY OF CHRIST
JESUS.

PHIL 1:3-6

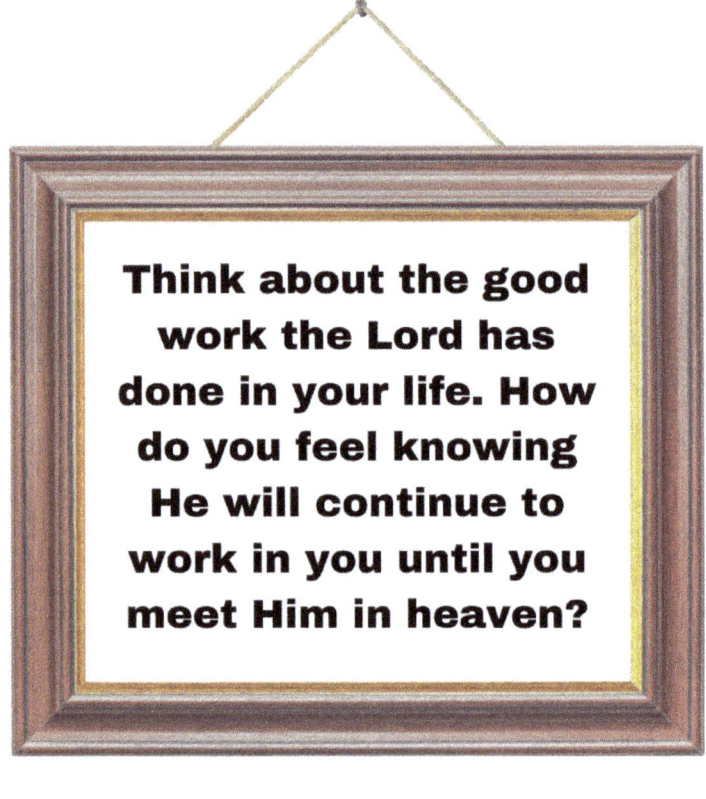

Think about the good work the Lord has done in your life. How do you feel knowing He will continue to work in you until you meet Him in heaven?

STOP...

JOURNAL TO THE LORD ABOUT WHAT THIS PROMISE MEANS TO YOU. WHY IS THIS PROMISE IMPORTANT?

ASK...

ASK THE LORD ABOUT HOW THIS PROMISE APPLIES TO YOUR LIFE RIGHT NOW. SPEAK FROM THE HEART ABOUT WHY YOU ARE ASKING.

OBEY...

HOW CAN I APPLY WHAT THE LORD HAS TOLD ME INTO MY LIFE CONSISTENTLY GOING FORWARD?

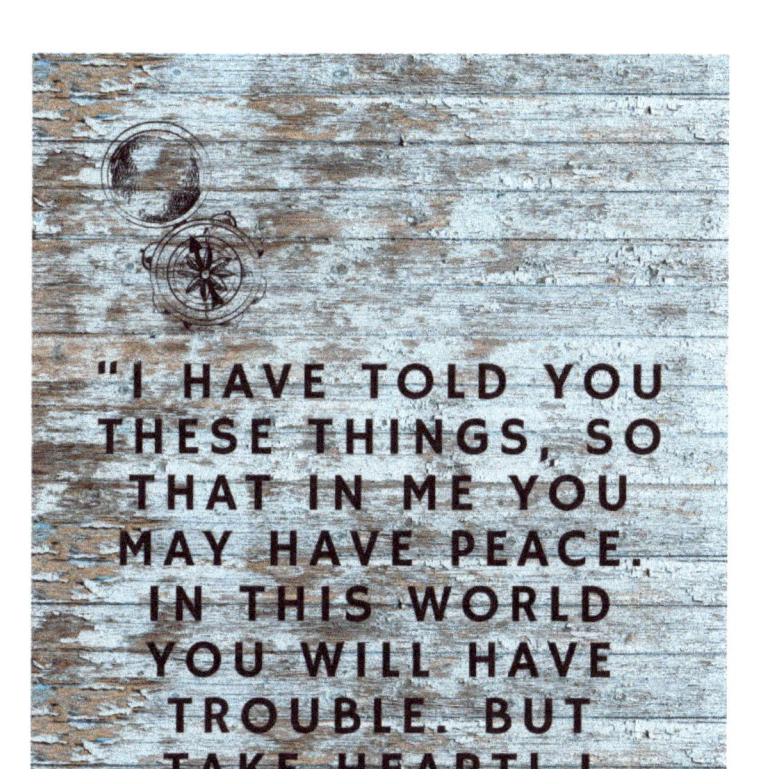

"I HAVE TOLD YOU
THESE THINGS, SO
THAT IN ME YOU
MAY HAVE PEACE.
IN THIS WORLD
YOU WILL HAVE
TROUBLE. BUT
TAKE HEART! I
HAVE OVERCOME
THE WORLD."

JOHN 16:33

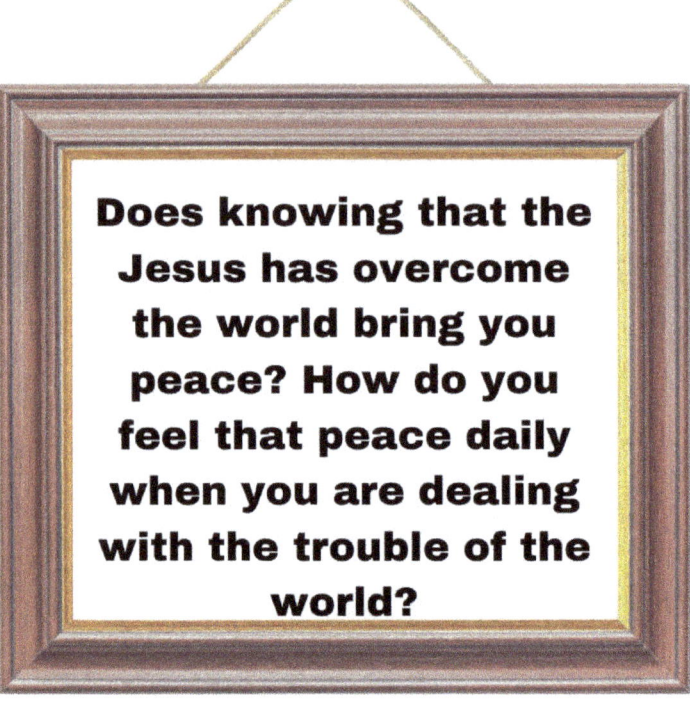

Does knowing that the Jesus has overcome the world bring you peace? How do you feel that peace daily when you are dealing with the trouble of the world?

STOP...

JOURNAL TO THE LORD ABOUT WHAT THIS PROMISE MEANS TO YOU. WHY IS THIS PROMISE IMPORTANT?

ASK...

ASK THE LORD ABOUT HOW THIS PROMISE APPLIES TO YOUR LIFE RIGHT NOW. SPEAK FROM THE HEART ABOUT WHY YOU ARE ASKING.

OBEY...

HOW CAN I APPLY WHAT THE LORD HAS TOLD ME INTO MY LIFE CONSISTENTLY GOING FORWARD?

GIVE THANKS TO THE LORD, FOR HE IS GOOD; HIS LOVE ENDURES FOREVER. 1 CHRONICLES 16:34

STOP...

JOURNAL TO THE LORD ABOUT WHAT THIS PROMISE MEANS TO YOU. WHY IS THIS PROMISE IMPORTANT?

ASK...

ASK THE LORD ABOUT HOW THIS PROMISE APPLIES TO YOUR LIFE RIGHT NOW. SPEAK FROM THE HEART ABOUT WHY YOU ARE ASKING.

OBEY...

HOW CAN I APPLY WHAT THE LORD HAS TOLD ME INTO MY LIFE CONSISTENTLY GOING FORWARD?

ABOUT THE AUTHOR

Dawn is an author and speaker on Biblical topics having worked with thousands of individuals across the globe on topics including relationships, marriage and hearing God's voice. She is the host of "Conquering Our Unseen Enemies" Podcast and as a lifelong world traveler, she is the YouTube host of "Life Journey with Dawn Simmons." Over the course of her life, she has visited numerous archaeological and biblical sites which fueled her passion to help individuals understand biblical history and how it relates to our lives today. With education and research in both Business and History, including 20 years of mentoring and teaching, Dawn's coaching methodology helps people to better understand the Bible and develop their relationship with Jesus. Dawn is a mother of 4 and lives with her husband in Ventura County California.

Connect with us!

For more resources on how to develop your relationship with the Lord using the **SALO** method, join the SALO Circle membership community at our website:

www.lovingconversationssalo.com

Contact us at:

contact@lovingconversationssalo.com

Follow us on Instagram:

lovingconversationssalo

Related Titles:

Loving Conversations: How to Pray and Hear God's Voice

ISBN: 978-1-960775-05-4

Loving Conversations Study Guide and Journal: How to Pray and Hear God's Voice
ISBN: 978-1-960775-06-1

God's Promises SALO Devotional

ISBN: 978-1-960775-07-8